Dramatis Personae

Poodle   A chicken

What?   A beagle

Sidney   A snail

Maybe   A mouse (the director)

Bizzie   A mouse (Maybe's assistant)

Dickinson   A wind monster

Burgull   A consonant monster

Gawk   An indignant desert bird

Vermeer   A painter

Author   Unknown

2

Royal Fireworks   Language Arts   by Michael Clay Thompson

Book 5 of the Poodle Series

Poodle
and the
Art of the Comma

Michael Clay Thompson

Illustrations by Christopher Tice

Royal Fireworks Press
UNIONVILLE, NEW YORK

October 2023

Copyright © 2023
Royal Fireworks Online Learning, Inc.
All Rights Reserved. No copying, reproduction, or electronic dissemination
of this book is permitted without the express written consent of the publisher.

Royal Fireworks Press
41 First Avenue, P.O. Box 399
Unionville, NY 10988-0399
(845) 726-4444
fax: (845) 726-3824
email: mail@rfwp.com
website: rfwp.com

ISBN: 978-1-63856-130-9

Publisher: Dr. T.M. Kemnitz
Editor: Jennifer Ault
Illustrator: Christopher Tice

This book features QR codes that link to audio of Michael Clay Thompson
narrating the text so that readers can follow along.

With special appreciation to my wife, Dr. Myriam Borges Thompson,
whose contributions of editing and literary sense have informed this book, as usual.

Printed and bound in Unionville, New York,
at the Royal Fireworks facility.   17oct23

local 363

Table of Contents

Dramatis Personae 1

Act One: Monsters 3

Act Two: The Echo 19

Act Three: Van Gogh 35

Act Four: Brueghel 61

Act Five: Miró 89

Act Six: Vermeer...................................... 113

End of Book Quiz 136

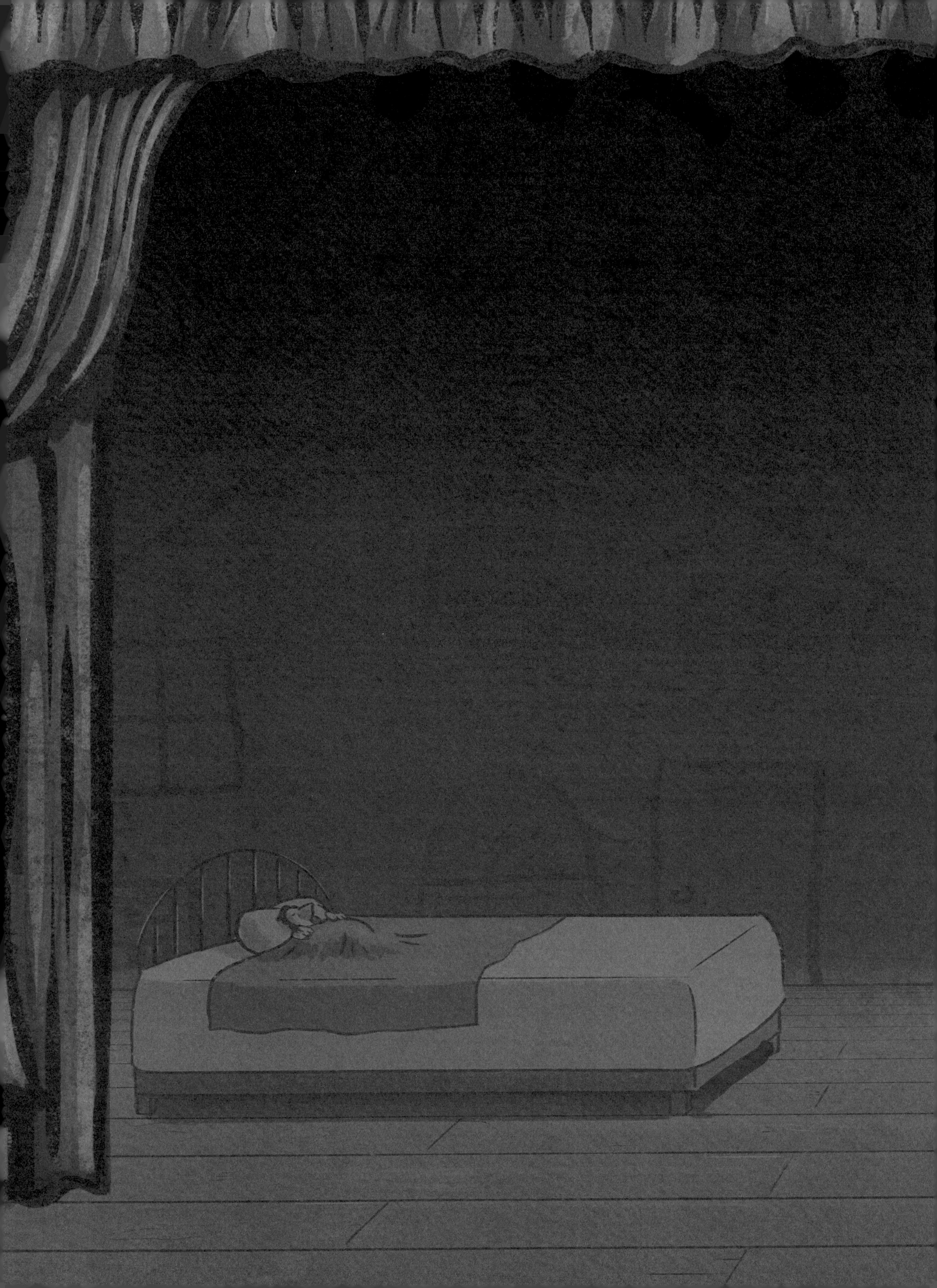

Act One:
Monsters

Through space and time he'd trekked,
and Poodle now was wrecked.
He'd crossed a gap.
What a flap.
He'd need a nap.

He snugged in bed, ducked his head,
pulled up his blankie, and closed his eyes.
But then....

He opened one eye. No, the other one.
He scanned left. He peeked right.
He listened.

Cautiously, he whispered to the quiet room,
"Are there any monsters under my bed?"

"Nope," came a low voice from below.
"Uh-uh, not here, nope," said another.
"Grbrno monssers, nohpp," said a third.

"Burgull! Is that you?" Poodle cried.
"Are you under my bed?"
He jumped to the floor
and spied some consonants under his bed.
Sure enough, that consonant monster was there.

"Grbr, nope here, grk," came the reply.
Typical Burgull.

"Burgull, you can't hide under my bed,
even if you are a consonant monster," Poodle said.

"Grbrburkk, help Poodle," came gurbly words.
"Burgull, guard Poodle."

Why had Burgull used that comma?
"Argh," Poodle said, like a pirate.
The comma? He didn't admire it.
"Burgull, who else is under there?"

"Not me, oooooh," came a blue voice,
which sounded like Dickinson.

"Me either, too, also, yup," came a voice, awkward,
like Gawk, the indignant desert bird.

5

"Burgull, help Poodle," came the burgly voice.

"Wait," said Poodle, "did you say,
'Burgull comma help Poodle'?"

"Grurburgk?" asked Burgull.

"Did you say comma?" asked Poodle.
"Between your subject and verb?"

"Grbrk?" Burgull was so confused.

"Burgull, come out of there."
Poodle could see some scratchy g's and k's
sticking out from under the bed.

There was a pitiful grk,
and Burgull crawled out, grking.

"Burgull," said Poodle, "you put a comma between your subject and your verb! You said, 'Burgull, help Poodle.' See that messy comma?"

"Grbrk?" came a confused gurp.

"Tell him, Gawk," said Poodle.

Silence.

Gawk, the indignant desert bird,
was under the bed too. Poodle *knew* it.
"Gawk, I *know* you're under there.
Come out and tell him.
You can do it," Poodle said.
"See to it.
Please tell Burgull.
Just review it.
Tell Burgull 'bout commas.
Go through it."

"Nope," came Gawk's voice.
"I'm not here."

Desert birds make things so difficult.

"Right. I *know* you're there," pressed Poodle.
"Tell him, Gawk. Please."

"Oh, all right, but I'm not here," said Gawk at last.
"Burgull, commas aren't herbs;
curb them; don't blurb 'em
between subjects and verbs.
Subjects and verbs go together,
like fluffs of a feather.
Instead of '**Burgull comma help Poodle**,'
just say, '**Burgull helps Poodle**.' See?
No comma between subjects and verbs."

To be fair, this was not a good topic
for a consonant monster. Poor thing.
Poodle began to explain once more, but....

"CUT! LIGHTS!" yelled Maybe,
the director, as she stormed onto the stage,
Bizzie scurrying behind,
trying to put something
in her pocket.

Maybe always *storms*. You remember.

Joe popped on the lights,
which griped and grumped above the stage.

"Stick to the script!" Maybe cried.
"Skip the trauma! No one hears a comma!
They're punctuation! Points, not joints!
You see 'em when you read 'em!"

"But I see the commas on this page,"
said Poodle. "I see sentences on our stage.
I read them. I see talk bubbles."

"Talk bubbles? Nonsense!" Maybe cried.
"This is a play; we hear it;
we don't see words. They're heard."

"Well, actually...," began the author,
his voice coming from somewhere.

"You stay out of this! Please!" said Maybe.
"You're the author. You're not a character."

There was a disgruntled *hmmph*
from somewhere.
Authors are somewhere.
No one knows where it is.
Authors are not *in* their books.
They hover, annoyingly,
like mosquitoes.

"You monsters," Maybe said
to the three monsters,
who had crawled out
and stood sheepishly in line.
"Don't mumble under the bed.
No mumbling! Speak your lines
like monstry monsters!
I need more *grump* and *crump*,
more *gawk* and *burgle*.
And no more comma nonsense!"

The monsters shook their clouds
and wings and consonants.

It's not easy being a monster.

Bizzie stood to the side,
by the curtain,
and Poodle, uncertain,
whispered to her, "What's your name?"

"I'm Bizzie," she said.
She looked at Poodle and smiled.

"I know you're busy," he replied,
"but what is your name?"

Before she could respond....

"Cut the lights!" yelled Maybe. "ACTION!"
And she stormed off the stage,
Bizzie flying behind,
blue whiz marks in pursuit.

There are always blue whiz marks,
but only animals see them. And monsters.

Joe cut the lights, and the stage
became its world.

From his somewhere,
the author wrote final sentences
for the chapter, such as this one.

"Wait!" Poodle said.
"Stop writing! Please! Where's What??"

The author stopped courteously. What?
What? was missing?

The monsters looked left together,
then right together,
and raised their hands together,
palms up, in group perplexity.
They'd been practicing.

(I know; none of them actually has *hands*.)

"What?!" Poodle called. What? did not answer.
Poodle's heart sank.

Act One Review:
The Subject/Verb Comma

At the heart of every sentence you speak or think, there is a two-part structure: **a subject and its verb**. The **subject** is the noun or pronoun that the sentence is about, and the **verb**, which we might call the simple **predicate**, is about the subject. The verb tells what the subject does or is.

See? Our thoughts (sentences) are beautifully simple.

The subject and its verb are a team. They work together. They are the nucleus of thought. They mean what they mean because they are together, and their teamwork is a key to clear thought, so we do not put anything between them if we can avoid it, including a comma, which would divide them.

No: The lurking monster, ate the whole beet.

Yes: The lurking monster ate the whole beet.

Our first comma rule is: **Avoid the subject/verb (s/v) comma.**

Act One Practice Sentences

For each sentence, write *yes* if the sentence is correct and *no* if the sentence is not correct.

1. Seven morby monsters, roared again.

2. The flubbely monster never jumped.

3. Burgull asked Poodle for a snack.

4. Burgull, heard sounds in the sky.

5. Poodle, explained the idea to Burgull.

6. Maybe asked Bizzie to cut the lights.

7. Maybe, directed the play again.

8. Gawk loved to fly in the clouds.

9. Gawk, loved to eat seven beets.

10. Poodle, explained commas to Burgull.

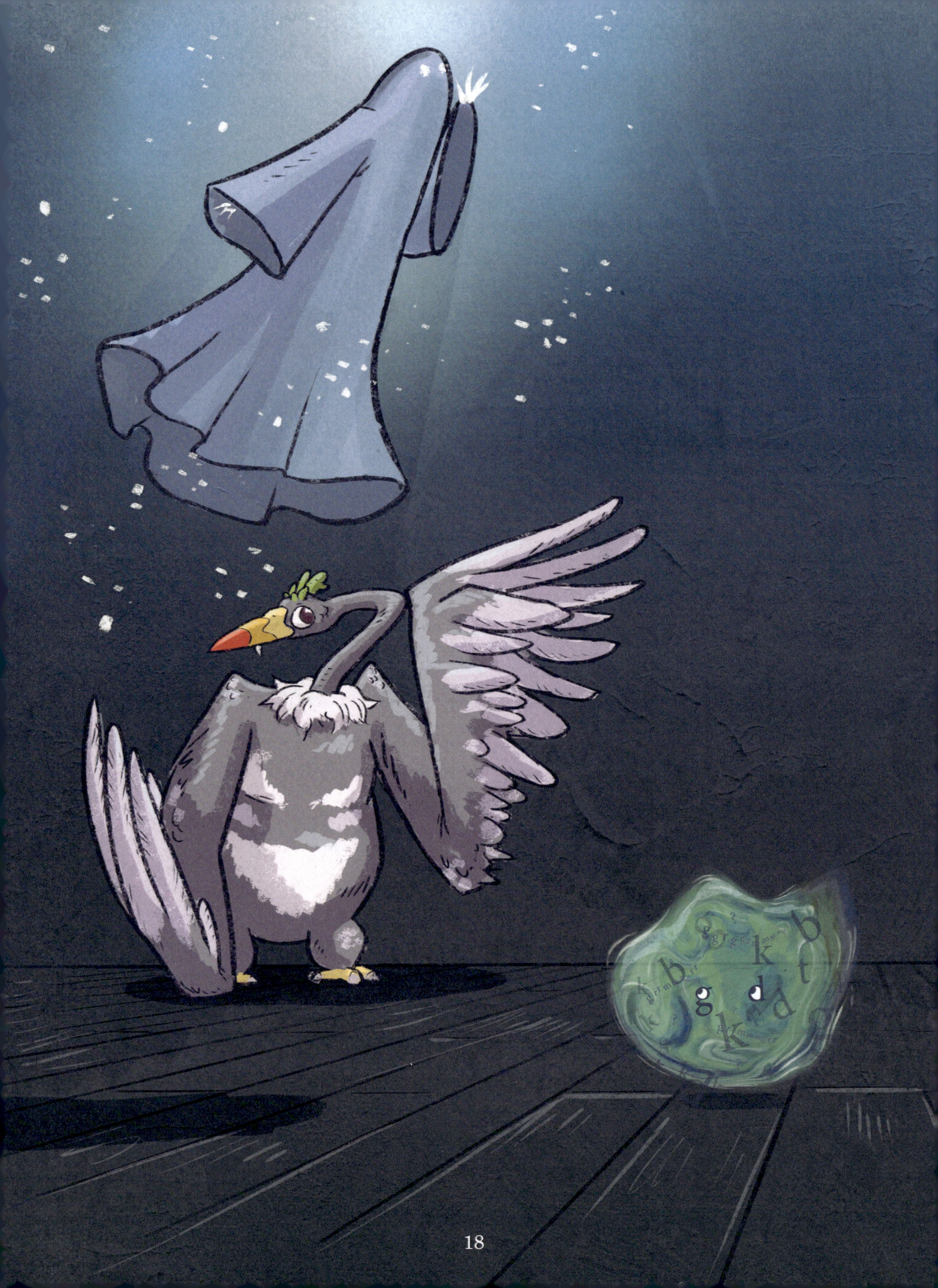

Act Two: The Echo

"What?!" Poodle called.
"What?!!"

Everyone listened
for What?'s barky *what-what-what!*

Poodle listened.

Burgull listened.

Dickinson, the Blue Mountain citizen,
lofted into the glisten and listened.

Gawk spread his wings
to funnel the sound and listened.
You know those desert birds.

Bizzie peeked out
from the curtain stage right
and listened. She looked back at Maybe.

The author got fidgety and fidgeted.
He didn't know where What? was either.
Authors can't know everything.

The children, high above the stage, listened.

Nothing.

"We have to find What?," Poodle said,
and he looked at the monsters.

Dickinson hovered again,
casting blue gleams o'er the team.
Gawk gawked hawkily.
Burgull's consonants got scratchier than ever.
Everyone understood.

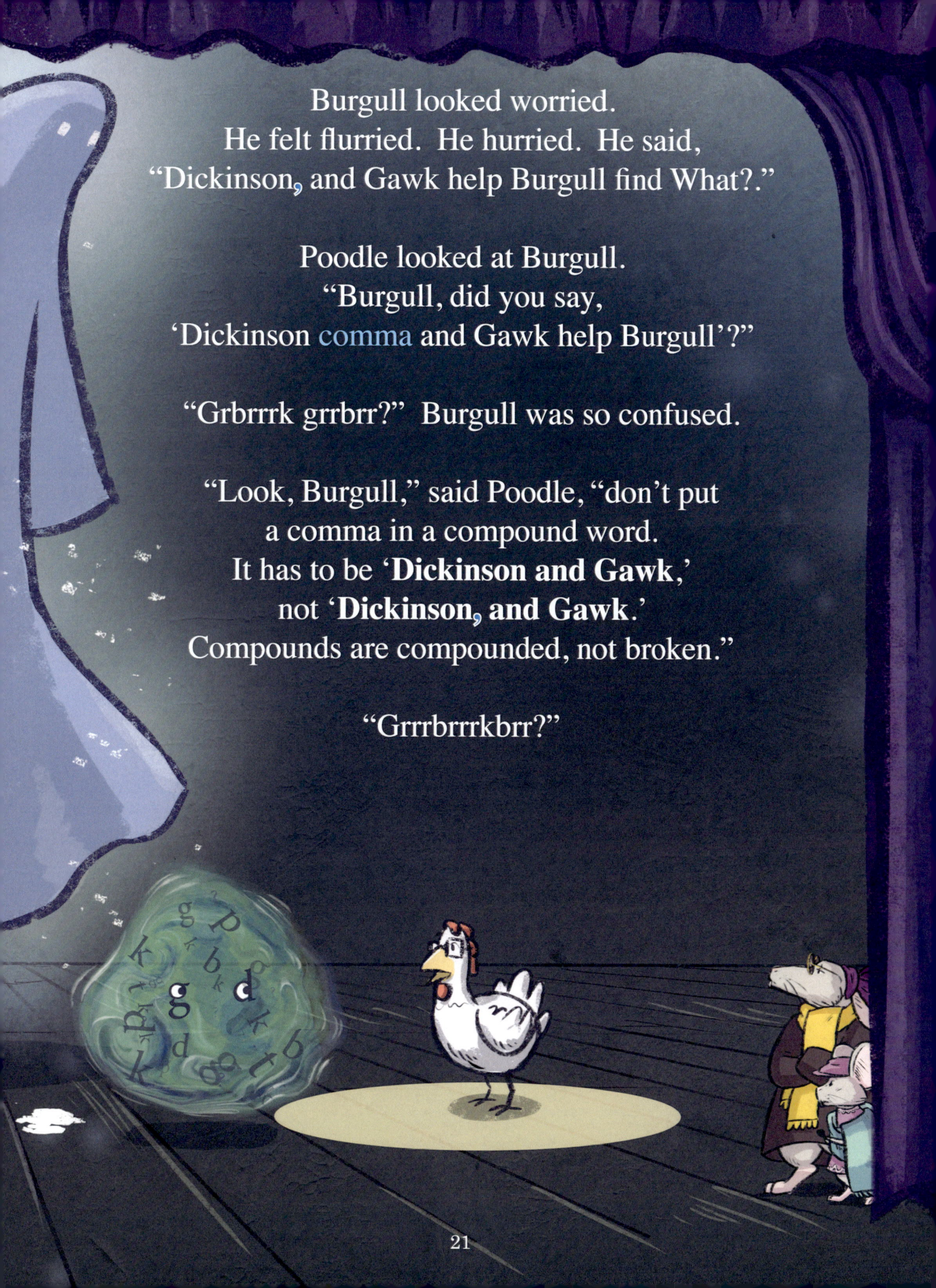

Burgull looked worried.
He felt flurried. He hurried. He said,
"Dickinson, and Gawk help Burgull find What?."

Poodle looked at Burgull.
"Burgull, did you say,
'Dickinson comma and Gawk help Burgull'?"

"Grbrrrk grrbrr?" Burgull was so confused.

"Look, Burgull," said Poodle, "don't put
a comma in a compound word.
It has to be '**Dickinson and Gawk**,'
not '**Dickinson, and Gawk**.'
Compounds are compounded, not broken."

"Grrrbrrrkbrr?"

This was too hard for Burgull.
Monsters don't know compounds.

"Burgull," Poodle began gently,
"in a compound noun,
such as raining *cats and dogs*,
we want the conjunction to join;
we don't want a comma
to break the compound. See?"

"Grrrbrrrk?"

Poodle sat down and put his beak
on his wing like a thinker.

"Tell him, Dickinson," said Poodle.
"Tell Burgull about compound words, please."

Dickinson looked dubious,
and his blue began to glow.
He flowed left, and swept slow,
and hummed *oh* in the air.

"Burgull," Dickinson whirred,
"when you have a **compound**—
two nouns such as ***cats and mice***,
or two verbs such as ***ran and jumped***,
or two adjectives such as ***red and blue***—
the conjunctions conjoin them.
Don't let commas crack them."

"Grbrrrkk?"

Dickinson looked at Poodle.
Poodle looked at Dickinson.
Gawk looked down.

"Enough," said Poodle. "Let's just find What?. We'll worry about **compound commas** later. Just remember: no subject/verb comma, and no compound word comma. Right?"

Burgull's countenance was confused. "Burgull search, and help Poodle," he said.

"No comma," said Poodle. "No comma in a compound verb."

"Grbrrkk?"

Everyone stopped and looked at the walls.

"So, let me think," said Poodle at last.
"I think Sidney could find What?.
Where's Sidney? We need Sidney—as usual.
She's fast enough to look everywhere."

Good idea. It was time
for the world's fastest snail
to lead the search.

"Sidney!" called Poodle. "Sidney!"

"Yes?" came her voice from back stage,
from some page behind the curtain.

"Sidney! We need you! What?'s missing!"

That's all it took.
Sidney was tired of waiting back there.
She was missing this whole book.

It was one of Sidney's grand entrances.
You know her.

There was a SCREECH and a WHIRRR,
and the whole page lifted into the air,
and the book rattled and clattered,
and a bump came from some chapter,
and the stage trembled,
and the lights skitchered,
and the curtain wiggled,
and *whooooosh!* came the whoosh,
and *poof!*, Sidney zapped, vaulting,
smack! in front of Poodle, BANG!,
a blur of whir stirring around her feet.
Not feet, exactly. You know. She's a snail.

"What's this?" asked Sidney. "What?'s gone?"

"Yes," said Poodle, and the three monsters
nodded their heads up, then down.
Together. They'd been practicing.

"Right," said Sidney, the action snail.
"Follow me!" And she bolted
toward the right side of the page,
and *whooooosh!*, she jumped
off of the page and was gone.
Just like that.

Burgull had forgotten
that they were on a page.

Everyone looked at each other, blinked,
and leaped after Sidney in a wink.
Their whiz marks whished over the brink.
Just like that.

Suddenly, the stage was silent.

Just like this.

Silence.
Except that two lights disagreed above the stage.
Snap. Crackle. Pop. Lights never get along.

Finally, a muffled g*rrff* came
from somewhere, and What?—of all dogs—
wandered, weaving, onto the stage,
his doggy feet making little pats, one to four.
He was groggy. His brain was soggy
from his nap behind the curtain.
"Where is everyone?" he yawned, uncertain.
"Hello?" he called.

"Hello?" came an echo from the shadow.

"Is anyone there?" What? called again.

"There?" asked the echo.

"Poodle?" called What?.

"Poodle? What's this?" asked the echo.
"You expect me to repeat everything?"

"What?" asked What?.
"You *have* to repeat everything.
You're an echo. It's your job."

"Job?" echoed the echo.
"Give me a break. I'll do a few words,
but I can't spend all day with you.
I have responsibilities."

"Okay," said What?.

"Okay," echoed the echo.

They understood each other.

The echo faded.

What? looked around.
The stage was now so silent,
except for the grumpy lights above,
and What? realized that his friends had left.
He knew what they'd done.
They'd jumped.

He'd catch them.
He padded over to the right margin,
peeked over the edge of the page
to see what was down there
(Nothing. He saw nothing.),
and jumped into the void.

Sometimes, he knew, you have to trust the author.
(The author wrote that.)

On the silent stage,
only What?'s blue whiz marks remained;
then they jumped too.
They weren't going to hang around.

As What? plummeted through space,
he thought he could see,
almost out of sight far below,
the blue whiz marks of his friends,
streaking after Poodle and the gang.

One little whiz mark had gotten lost
and was squeaking around the page,
from the left margin to the right,
looking for its gang.
It was so upset.

What? dropped right past him.
"Follow me!" he called back,
and the little whiz mark whirled
and chased after him.

Act Two Review:
The Compound Word Comma

The first rule we learned about commas is not to let commas break subjects from verbs. It should be *Joe is the stage hand*, not *Joe, is the stage hand*.

In Act Two we discover another important rule: Do not let a comma break a **compound word**. A compound word is a double word joined by the conjunction *and* or *or*. Some compound words are *up and down*, *ran and jumped*, *black and blue*, *you or me*, *yes and no*. Any of the eight parts of speech can be joined into a compound.

The key to the idea is that, like subjects and verbs, the two words of the compound work together. We want them to be together because we are saying something about them both. They make a **unity**. For example, you could use a compound noun as a direct object: *Burgull ate **beets and carrots.***

So, just as we saw the unity of the subject and verb, now we see the unity of compound words. Clear thinking involves unity.

Act Two Practice Sentences

For each sentence, write *yes* if the sentence is correct and *no* if the sentence is not correct.

1. Burgull, and Poodle ate no beets.

2. Burgull, ate no beets.

3. Burgull and Poodle, ate no beets.

4. Burgull ate no beets.

5. Burgull and Poodle ate no beets.

6. Burgull ate beets, and carrots.

7. Burgull ate beets and carrots.

8. Gawk, flew over the land.

9. Gawk flew over the land.

10. Gawk and Burgull, flew over the land.

34

Act Three: Van Gogh

Far below the falling What?,
the friends dropped past the pages,
and the whiz marks streaked blue,
and the lines flew like birds—
blue blurs of true words, herds—
and way down there
the friends saw a landing zone
rushing up, and they braced for the *poof*.

Landings always say *poof*.

The friends fell, and fell, and
then *poof!*, they landed smack
in a different version
of the world.

They shook themselves
and gained their footing
and collected their wits—most of them—
and the new world whirled.

"Here," said Sidney, looking around.
"We'll search here. What? might be near."

Burgull and Dickinson and Gawk
gave her a *yep* in unison.
They'd been practicing.

But before they could even begin,
they stood and stared
because this world was different—
different from any world they had seen.

They had landed in a painting.

A painting?

How can you land in a painting? Well....

Can you be in a book? Yes.
Can you be in a play? Yes.
Can you be in a poem? Yes.
Can you be in a painting? Oh.

They stood below a starry night
in a landscape washed in blue.
Blue hills rose to the right,
dark hills rose to the night,
night whirled in the height,
and stars curled as the sky whorled,
and lines of white whisked from the left,
and cypress trees groped up,
and the heavens opened to a curving sky.
The colors were shocking.

Wow.

There was nothing like it—
as though the whole universe were alive,
and the stars were intelligent,
and everything understood everything.

The paint was dabbed in strong strokes
of pure color, bold brush marks—magical.

"Where are we?"
squawked Gawk, shocked.

"I remember this," whispered Poodle.
"It's a Van Gogh." (*Gogh* sounds like *go*.)
"We landed in a Van Gogh painting."

"**Burgull, like colors**," said Burgull.

"No comma," said Poodle. "Say, '**Burgull likes** colors.'"

"Grgbgrkk?"

"No subject/verb comma, Burgull, please," said Poodle.

"Grrbrrk," said Burgull. "**Poodle, and Gawk** help Burgull."

"No compound comma," said Gawk. "Just say, '**Poodle and Gawk**.'"

Burgull was so confused.

Gawk stepped closer to explain, but Burgull said, "Grbr-ouch."

"Sorry," said Gawk. "I didn't mean to step on your consonant."
Gawk had stepped on Burgull's *g*.

It's not funny.

The friends gazed
at this blue heaven, this starry night
with Van Gogh strokes of pure color.
It was as though the Gogh-world moved,
and the streams of colors carried a current.

The painting they stood in
seemed to flow over them
like a flood of sparkles.

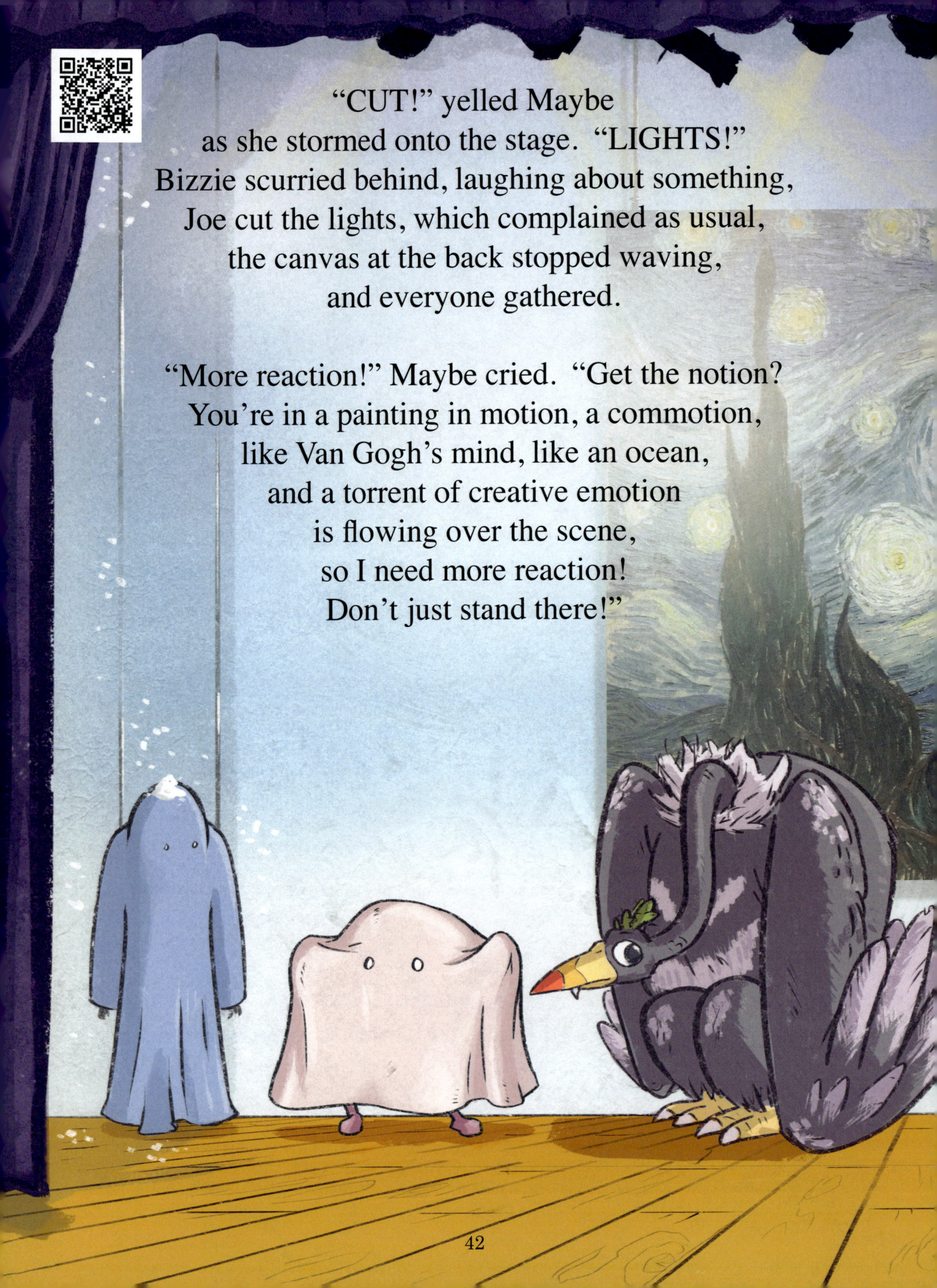

"CUT!" yelled Maybe
as she stormed onto the stage. "LIGHTS!"
Bizzie scurried behind, laughing about something,
Joe cut the lights, which complained as usual,
the canvas at the back stopped waving,
and everyone gathered.

"More reaction!" Maybe cried. "Get the notion?
You're in a painting in motion, a commotion,
like Van Gogh's mind, like an ocean,
and a torrent of creative emotion
is flowing over the scene,
so I need more reaction!
Don't just stand there!"

Poodle edged toward Bizzie.
She was making him dizzy.
"What's your name?" he whispered.

"I'm Bizzie," she said, and she smiled at him.

"I know you're busy," he said,
"but what's your name?"

Before Bizzie could reply,
Maybe yelled, "ACTION! REACTION!"
and stormed off stage. Bizzie grabbed the script
and hurried after Maybe,
and their blue whiz marks dashed after them.

Joe cut the lights,
the stage became the world,
and the Van Gogh sky unfurled.

The friends stood once more, staring,
gazing up at the starry night
with its blue-colored cosmos.

Somehow, Van Gogh's strokes
of pure color seemed more real than real, vivid,
as though each brush stroke were alive,
and Van Gogh's streams of creative meaning
flowed into their hearts.

The audience gasped.

Children, high above the book,
put their thoughts down and looked.

The author forgot what he was about to write.
Something about the night...
as though Van Gogh were displaying
the hidden colors of the truth.

Even Sidney stopped to gaze.

Burgull gurbulled,
"Burgull like burple, blue and green."

"Burgull," said Poodle,
"you need a comma in your list.
It isn't '**burple, blue and green**';
it's '**purple, blue, and green**.'
Put a comma before that **list** conjunction,
please. It's called an *Oxford comma*
or sometimes a *serial comma*.

"Grbkr?" Burgull was so confused.

"Look," Poodle said, "here are some messes:

Burgull, ate snacks.
Burgull, and Gawk ate stacks.
Poodle saw cows, oxen and yaks.

"Here is how they should be:

Burgull ate snacks.
Burgull and Gawk ate stacks.
Poodle saw cows, oxen, and yaks.

"See?" said Poodle. "No commas between subjects and verbs, no compound commas, but do put an Oxford comma in a list."

Before they could discuss commas further,
Sidney grew impatient.
She wanted to find What?.
"Right," she said, "but let's find What?.
He's not here."

It was true.
The Van Gogh colors curled,
and the world whirled,
but What? was nowhere to be seen.

Sidney did not fool around. You know her.
She zapped to the right margin,
peeked over the edge, and jumped,
and her blue whiz marks leaped too.
They had to hurry because she was fast.

Everyone else leaped after Sidney.
What choice did they have?

48

49

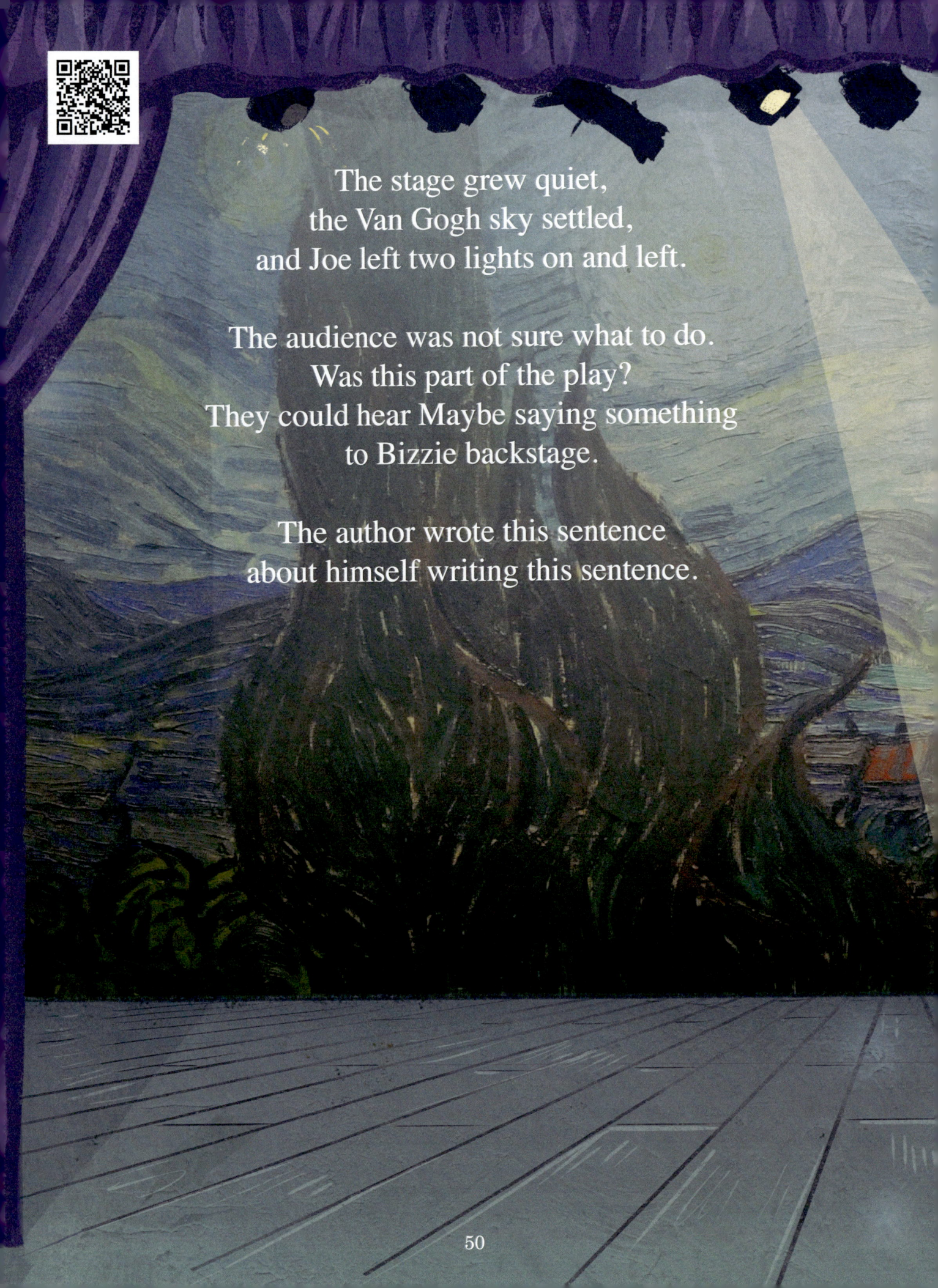

The stage grew quiet,
the Van Gogh sky settled,
and Joe left two lights on and left.

The audience was not sure what to do.
Was this part of the play?
They could hear Maybe saying something
to Bizzie backstage.

The author wrote this sentence
about himself writing this sentence.

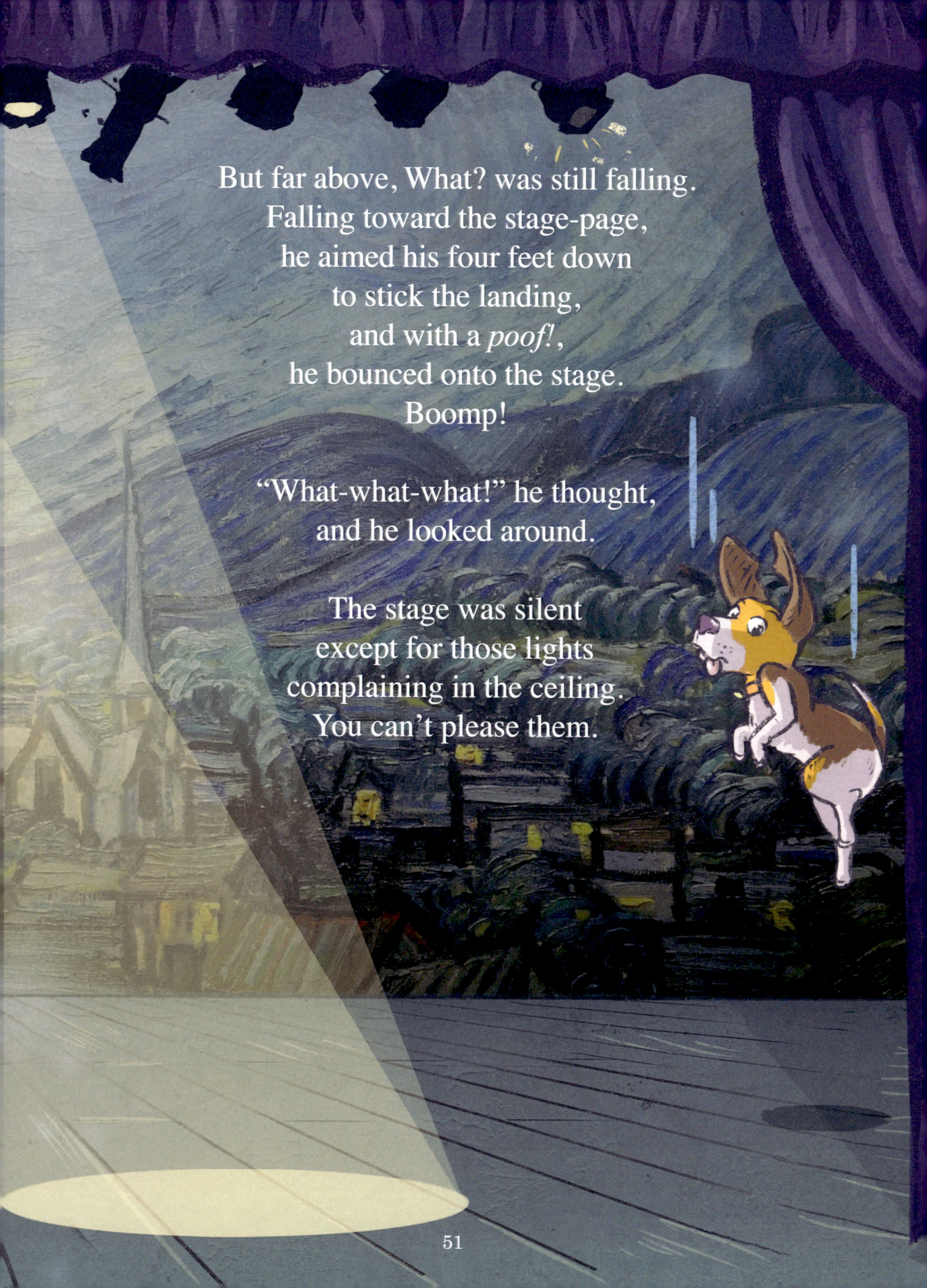

But far above, What? was still falling.
Falling toward the stage-page,
he aimed his four feet down
to stick the landing,
and with a *poof!*,
he bounced onto the stage.
Boomp!

"What-what-what!" he thought,
and he looked around.

The stage was silent
except for those lights
complaining in the ceiling.
You can't please them.

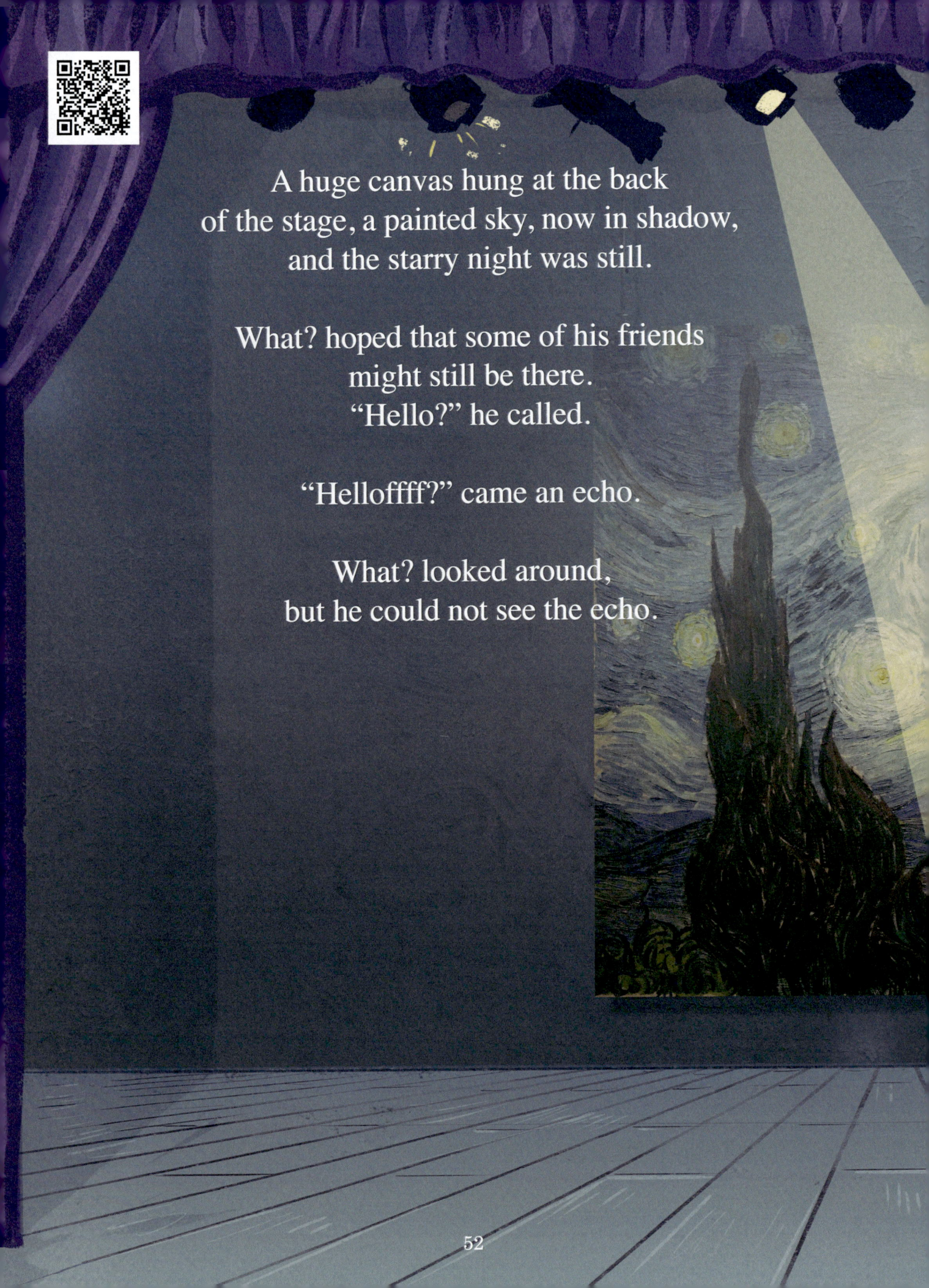

A huge canvas hung at the back
of the stage, a painted sky, now in shadow,
and the starry night was still.

What? hoped that some of his friends
might still be there.
"Hello?" he called.

"Helloffff?" came an echo.

What? looked around,
but he could not see the echo.

"Who's there?" cried What?.

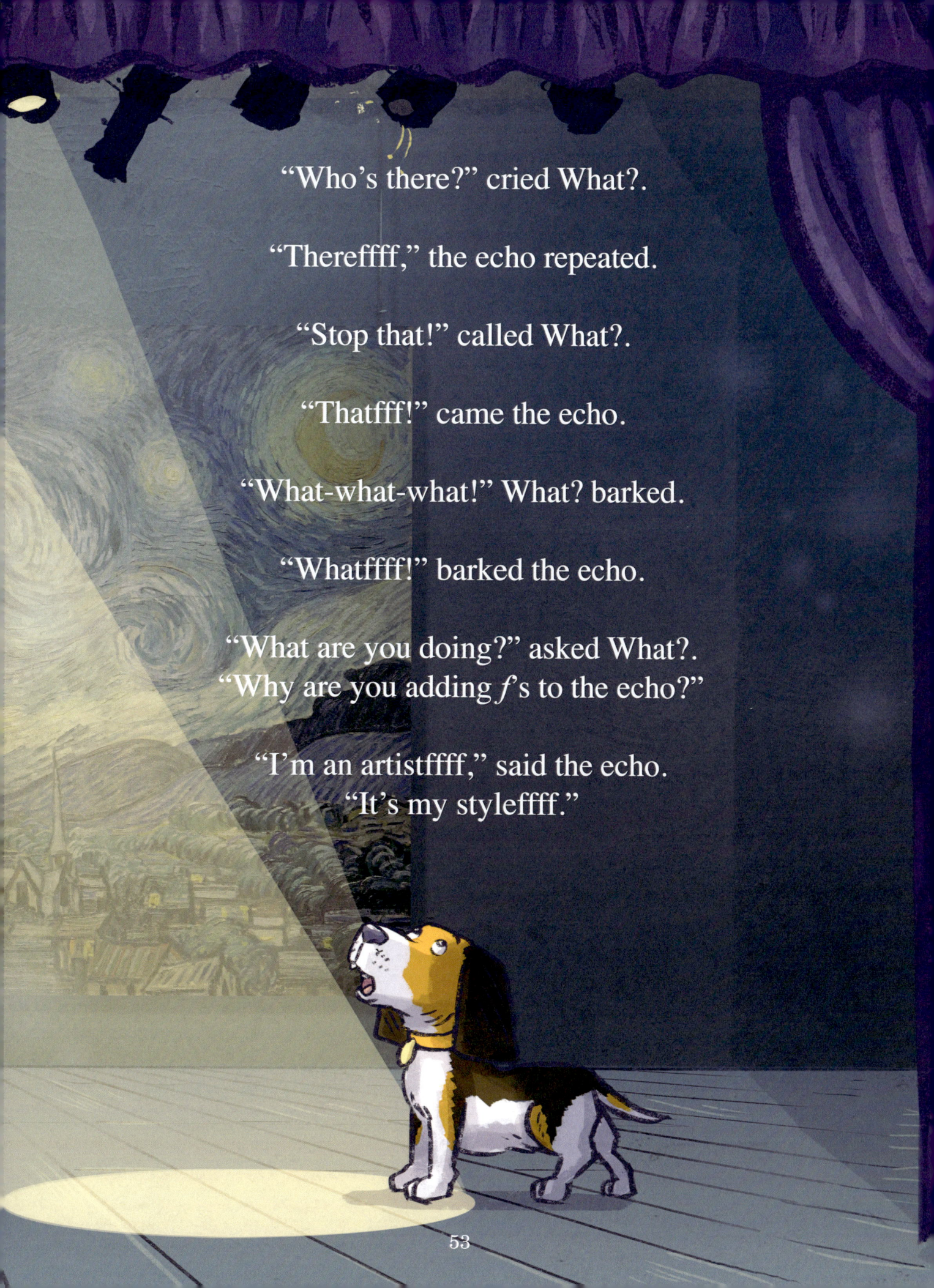

"Thereffff," the echo repeated.

"Stop that!" called What?.

"Thatfff!" came the echo.

"What-what-what!" What? barked.

"Whatffff!" barked the echo.

"What are you doing?" asked What?. "Why are you adding *f*'s to the echo?"

"I'm an artistffff," said the echo. "It's my styleffff."

"But you didn't add *f*'s in the last chapter,"
said What?. "Why are you adding *f*'s now?"

"Meffff?" asked the echo. "That wasn't meffff.
That was the dull echo you met up above.
I like *f*'s in my echoesffff."

"But those aren't echoes!" cried What?.
"That isn't how it works!
There are rules about echoes."

"Rulesfff?!" cried the echo.
"Are you seriousfff? RULES??? Fffff!!!"

"Oh, brother," said What?,
but before he could continue,
Maybe stormed out from the curtain stage left.
Bizzie hurried after, her hand on her hat.

"CUT!" cried Maybe. "This can't go on!
This scene is the no-play in a play
in a book in a poem, I say,
and you cannot argue with echoes.
Author, are you responsible for this mess?"

"Well," came the author's voice from somewhere,
"I wrote their words, but—"

"Nope," said Maybe. "It won't work.
We have to follow the friends.
We can't shirk. They left the Van Gogh,
and they're off to a different world
with its own quirks,
so please write that chapter."

"Well, all right," said the author,
but before he could continue,
Maybe glared at the silent stage,
cried, "ACTION!" and stormed away.
Bizzie ran after her.

The stage was silent once more.

What? looked around.
The starry night hung, a lifeless canvas,
in shadow at the back of the stage.
What? tried to imagine what it had looked like
when that sky was real.

He crept to the right margin,
peeked over, *grrffed*, and jumped.

His blue whiz marks watched him jump
and leaped after him.
They have to. You know that.

Silence invaded the stage,
and the echo had nothing to repeat.
It sat down, waiting.

Act Three Review:
The Oxford Comma

We have learned two comma rules already, and they both make sentences beautiful and clear. The first rule is to **keep the subject and its verb together** and not let a comma divide them. The second rule is to **keep compound words together** because they compound the idea. They make a unity.

Now we discover a new rule. Some writers do not follow this rule, but we will because it is beautiful and clear. This rule concerns the **Oxford comma**, which lets us put a comma before the conjunction in a list. It is a good idea.

Burgull was hungry, confused, and curious.

The comma before the *and* in the list is the Oxford comma, which is sometimes called a *serial comma*. Notice that a **compound** has two items, such as ***beets and carrots***, and does not use a comma. A **list** has three or more items, such as ***blue, green, and yellow***, and does use commas.

Act Three Practice Sentences

For each sentence, write *yes* if the sentence is correct and *no* if the sentence is not correct.

1. The new idea, was interesting.

2. The idea was different.

3. Burgull ate beets, tomatoes and carrots.

4. Burgull ate beets, tomatoes, and carrots.

5. Poodle ate beets, and corn.

6. Burgull ate beets and sandwiches.

7. Burgull, ate beets and sandwiches.

8. Gawk saw dogs, cats, and snails.

9. Gawk liked dogs, and cats.

10. Gawk, and he, ate leaves, roots and shoots.

grggr grggr grmmgrr
ggrgg ggrgg grmmgrr

g   d

Act Four: Brueghel

Far below the falling What?,
the friends flew too,
their whiz marks blue, rambunctious, new,
past pages and chapters, past nouns and bunches,
past rhymes and crunches and short conjunctions,
past verbs and punctuations.

As the friends fell from the Van Gogh,
commas flew like bees.
You couldn't avoid them.
Some commas squeezed
between subjects and verbs.
Buzz buzz. It was terrible.
It was a comma swarm.

One comma broke a compound noun
and had to be escorted off the page.
We can't have that.

As the friends dropped,
their blue whiz marks chased them,
puffing to keep up.

Whiz marks try to imitate shadows,
which stick like glue,
but that's a tall order.

As the friends dropped, the bottom rushed up,
and they aimed their feet (or consonants)
toward the landing zone, braced for impact,
and *poof!*, landed in a different world.

A different different world.

This was no Van Gogh.

They had fallen four centuries
and had landed in a frozen vista,
a gray scene of sixteenth-century Belgium,
a snowy landscape near Antwerp,
alive with busy people
swarming in all directions
like ants.

"Where is this?" asked Sidney.

The shivering monsters looked
at the land in the dead of winter
and at buildings stretching to the horizon
and saw crowds of crowdy people
skating on ice, slipping on ice,
buying food, **and** having fun.

(See the Oxford comma in that list?)

It was a winter world, shrouded in snow.
The brooks were frozen.
People crowded around fires,
talking, laughing, and joking.

In the trees there were crows.
Every child sees those.

Everyone was cold.
Burgull's old consonants rattled.
The monsters shivered in unison.
They'd been practicing.

"Where are we?" asked Sidney.

"I know where we are," said Poodle, shivering. "We're in a Brueghel."

"Broigull?" asked Burgull.

"It's spelled *B-r-u-e-g-h-e-l*," Poodle explained. "It's a painting by Pieter Brueghel, the Elder. He painted crows in his trees."

One of the crows lifted off its branch and flapped over their heads, its shadow following.

Dickinson had heard of Brueghel, but Burgull and Gawk had not.

As they shivered in this frozen landscape,
they knew they were not looking *at* a painting;
they were *in* it. They knew because
the icy wind blew their hair.
Or feathers. Or consonants.

Poodle scanned the land.
He thought about their long adventure.
The Van Gogh had shown
the deep secret colors of the world,
but this Brueghel was different.
It was a gray snow-world.
It wasn't about color;
it was about people living
in the bigness of the world.

And the painting was like a time machine,
showing a world of long ago
but with people just like us.
Talking to friends. Getting food.
Modern people in an old world.

And Poodle noticed something else.
The painting was not a portrait of a face.
It was crawling with people—everywhere.
It was about the crowd, about them all,
acting as one, like monsters.

It was reassuring, somehow, to know
that there were so many things to do,
so much fun to have.
The painting hummed with a love of life.

Poodle liked it.
He liked these busy people.
He liked this frosty Brueghel.
It was a different way to think.
It is nice, Poodle thought,
to have different ways to think.
He knew that he did not want
to be trapped forever
in his same old thoughts.

Sidney saw Poodle lost in thought, dazed.
She was unfazed. She raised her chin
and looked at Poodle.

"That Poodle," she thought, "what a thinker."
But then she cried, "Back to business!
It's a big scene. What? could be anywhere."

Everyone still stood lost in a trance,
taking in the busy, cold world,
but Sidney said, "Stop dreaming.
Let's search for What?."

As usual, Sidney was right.
You know her.

So off they went.

Poodle and Dickinson
searched the buildings
and the vast snow shroud.
Gawk and Burgull scanned the crowd.
Sidney, proud, zapped aloud,
peeking into every crevice,
zooming like a lawn mower,
and leaving a puffpuff trail.

No luck.

"What?!" called Poodle. No answer.
The crowd of busy people looked at him.
They'd never seen a talking chicken.
Not in the Netherlands.

Brueghel's paintings have few chickens.

A man stepped from the crowd.
"What is it you want?" he asked.

"Yes," said Poodle. "It is. I want What?."

"That's what I asked," said the man.
"You want what?"

"Yes," said Poodle. "Have you seen him?"

"Seen who?" asked the man.

"What?," said Poodle. "Have you seen What??"

The man blinked and looked confused.
"Seen what?" he tried again.

"Have you seen What??" asked Poodle.

"That's what I asked," said the man.

"Thank you," said Poodle.

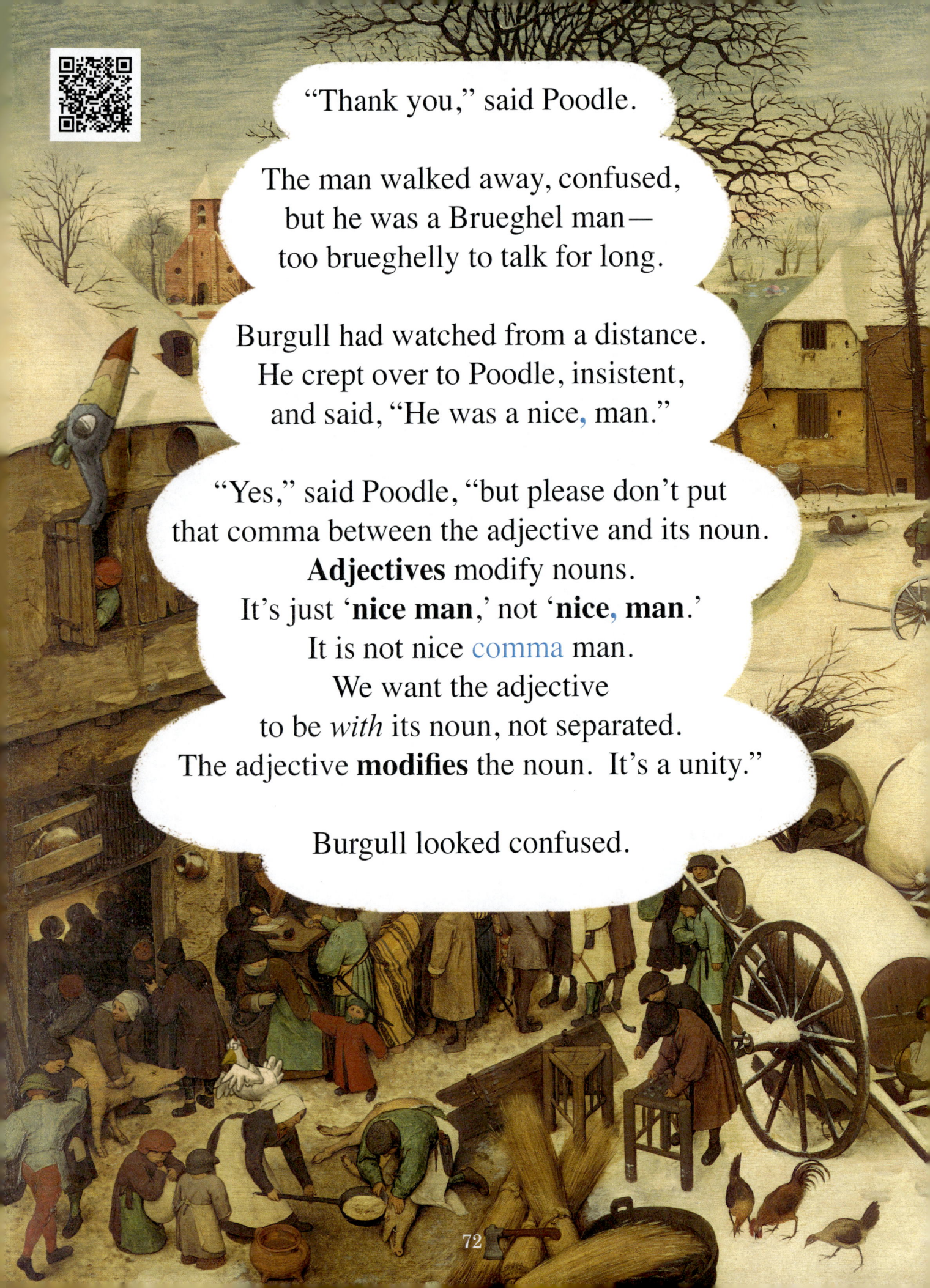

The man walked away, confused,
but he was a Brueghel man—
too brueghelly to talk for long.

Burgull had watched from a distance.
He crept over to Poodle, insistent,
and said, "He was a nice, man."

"Yes," said Poodle, "but please don't put
that comma between the adjective and its noun.
Adjectives modify nouns.
It's just '**nice man**,' not '**nice, man**.'
It is not nice comma man.
We want the adjective
to be *with* its noun, not separated.
The adjective **modifies** the noun. It's a unity."

Burgull looked confused.

And so it went.
They kept trying.
Everyone spent the day flying,
searching the Brueghel,
searching the crowds,
searching the buildings,
spying the trees
and the frozen brooks.

No What?.
He just wasn't there.

Sidney was about to call for a new search,
and she edged toward the margin for a jump,
but suddenly Maybe stormed out
from behind the curtain,
Bizzie hurrying behind.

"CUT!" Maybe cried. "LIGHTS!"
Joe turned on the stage lights, those grouches,
and the gray Brueghel world
dissolved into a wooden stage.

The actors gathered around.

"I need urgency!" Maybe cried. "Please!
What? has now been lost for two paintings.
I need you to look worried! Flurried!
Poodle, you stand to the right,
monsters to the left,
Sidney right here."

Poodle snuck a look at Bizzie.
"What's your name?" he whispered.

She looked at him quizzically.
"I'm Bizzie," she said,
but before she could continue,
Maybe cried, "ACTION!"
and Bizzie darted behind her,
vanishing behind the curtain stage right.

Poodle was puzzled.

Burgull looked at Poodle.
"Poodle a good, chicken," he said.

"Yes," said Poodle,
"but please do not forget your verb,
and do not put a comma
between an adjective and its noun.
It is '**good chicken**,' not '**good, chicken**.' See?
Instead of '**Poodle a good, chicken**,'
say, '**Poodle is a good chicken**.' See?"

"Grbrffrr?" asked Burgull.

What? was not in the gray Brueghel.
They had checked.
It was time to look elsewhere.
Speedy Sidney led the way, as we expect,
and off the page she jumped,
followed by monsters, and Poodle,
and their whiz marks, unaided.
The snow world faded
into a wooden stage.

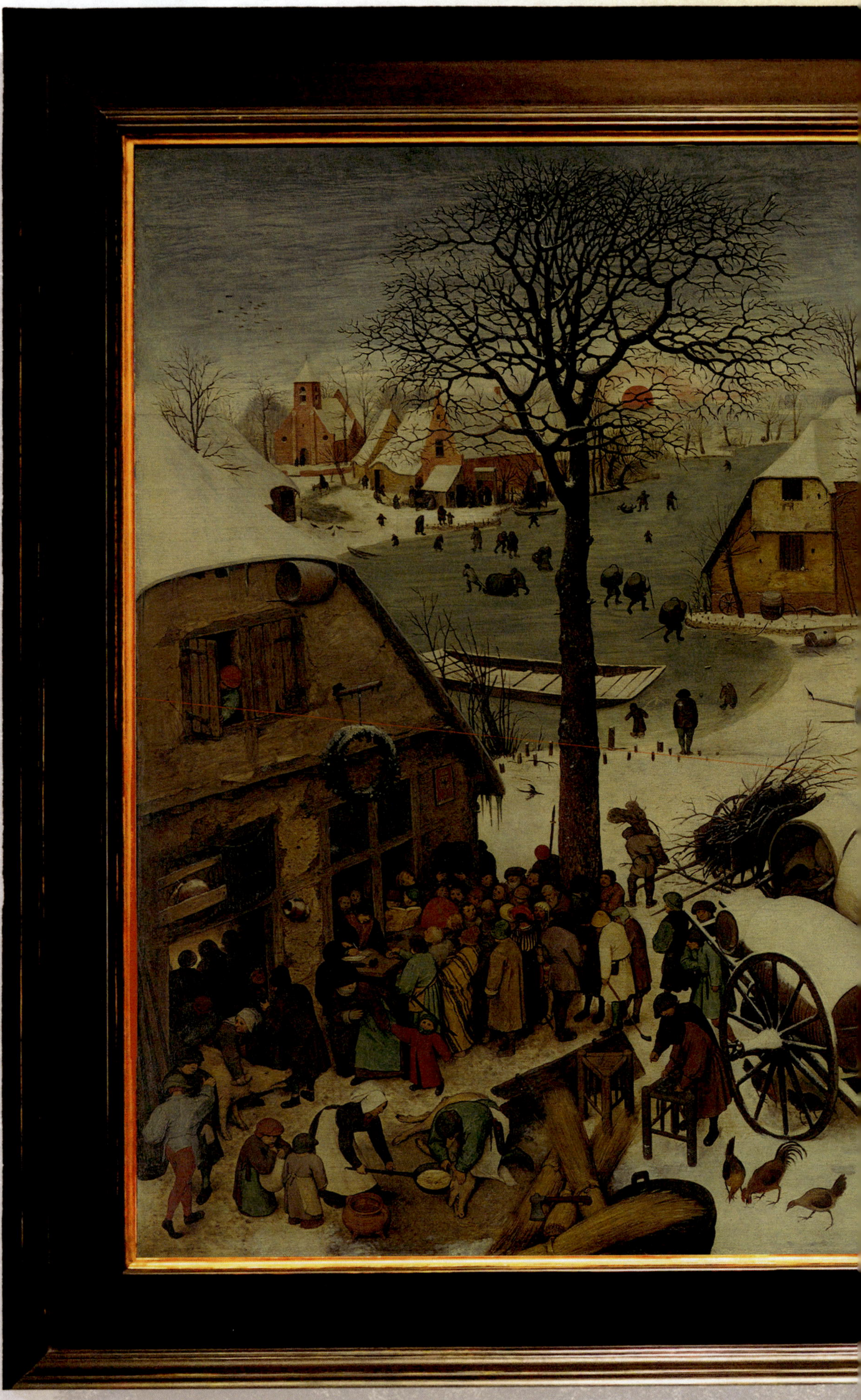

79

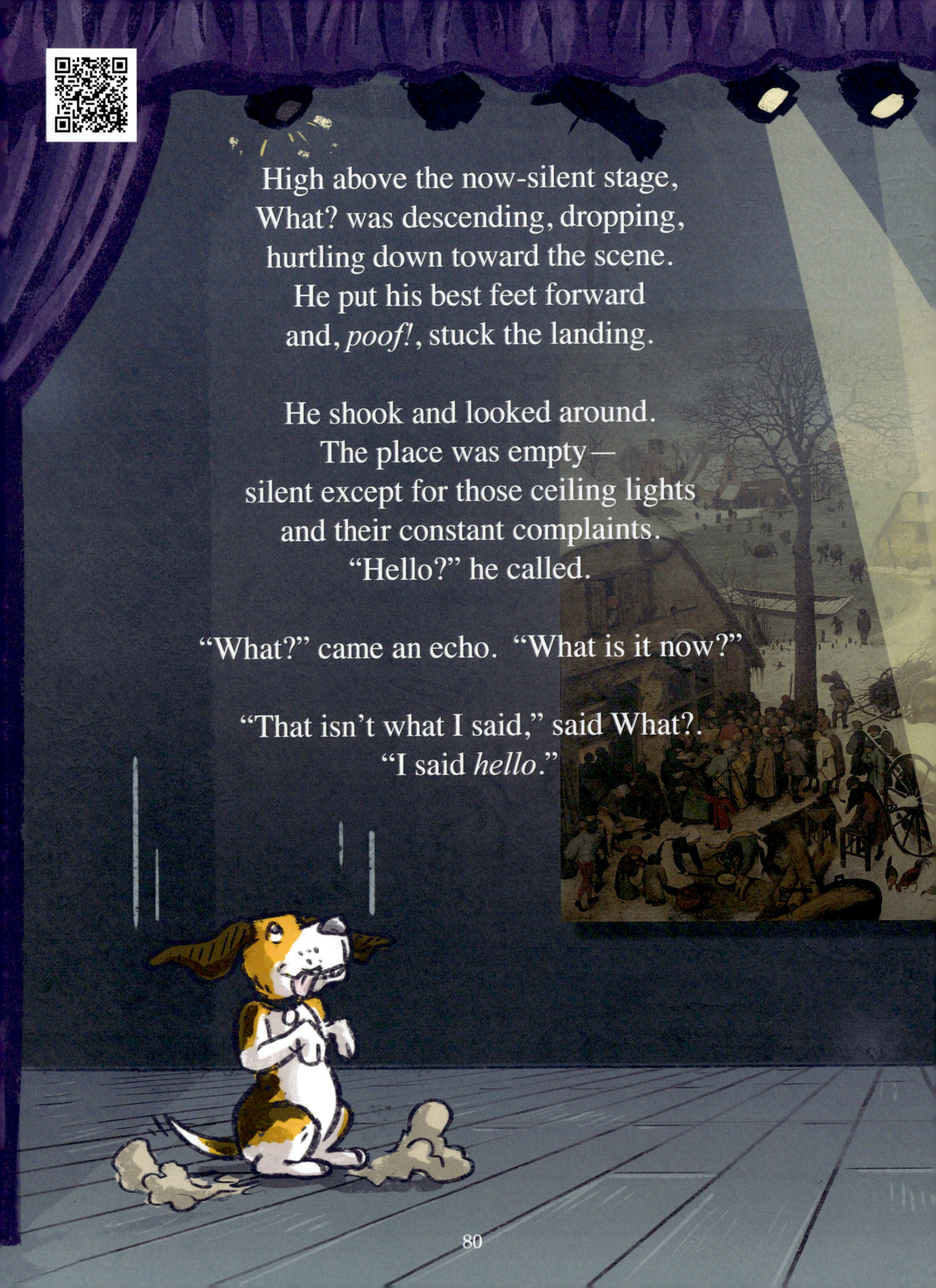

High above the now-silent stage,
What? was descending, dropping,
hurtling down toward the scene.
He put his best feet forward
and, *poof!*, stuck the landing.

He shook and looked around.
The place was empty—
silent except for those ceiling lights
and their constant complaints.
"Hello?" he called.

"What?" came an echo. "What is it now?"

"That isn't what I said," said What?.
"I said *hello*."

"So?" the echo replied. "What do you want?"

"You're my echo," said What?.
"You repeat me! Say *hello*!"

"I'm tired of that," said the echo.
"Just tell me what you want."

"But echoes repeat what they hear," said What?.
"That's your job. You're an echo!"

The echo sighed.
"What if it were *your* job," she tried,
"and all day you had to repeat dog words?"

What? had never thought of that.

"Look," said What?,
"was that you in the Van Gogh,
adding *f*'s to everything?"

"You mean like *thisfffff*?"

"Yes."

"No, that was my colleague," said the echo.
"He's an artist—so creative.
I'm independent. I'm me. I say what I want."

"Then you're not an echo," said What?.

"Of course I'm an echo," said the echo.
"Do you see me?"

"Well, no."

"Well, no. Exactly. I echo when I want."

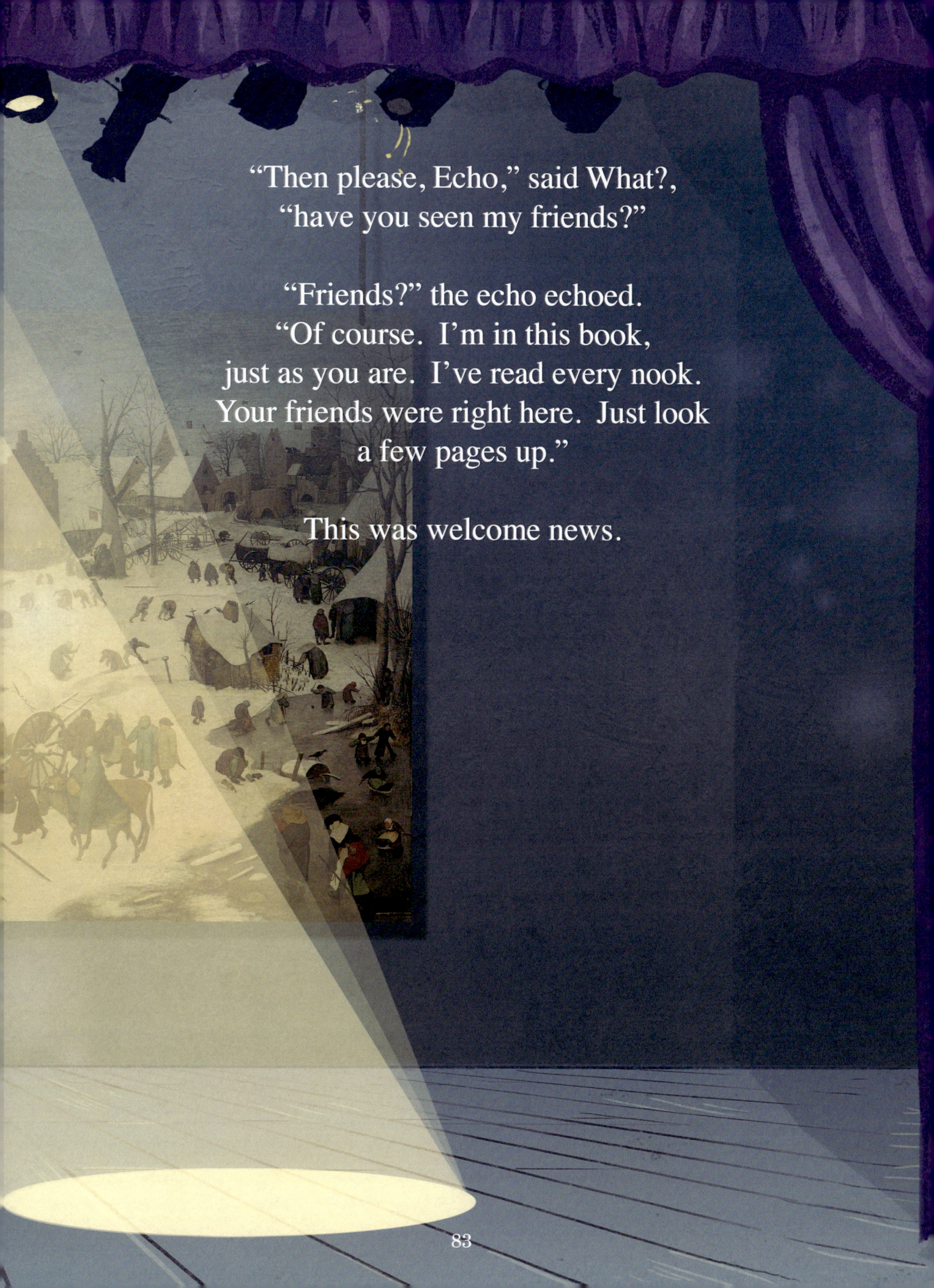

"Then please, Echo," said What?,
"have you seen my friends?"

"Friends?" the echo echoed.
"Of course. I'm in this book,
just as you are. I've read every nook.
Your friends were right here. Just look
a few pages up."

This was welcome news.

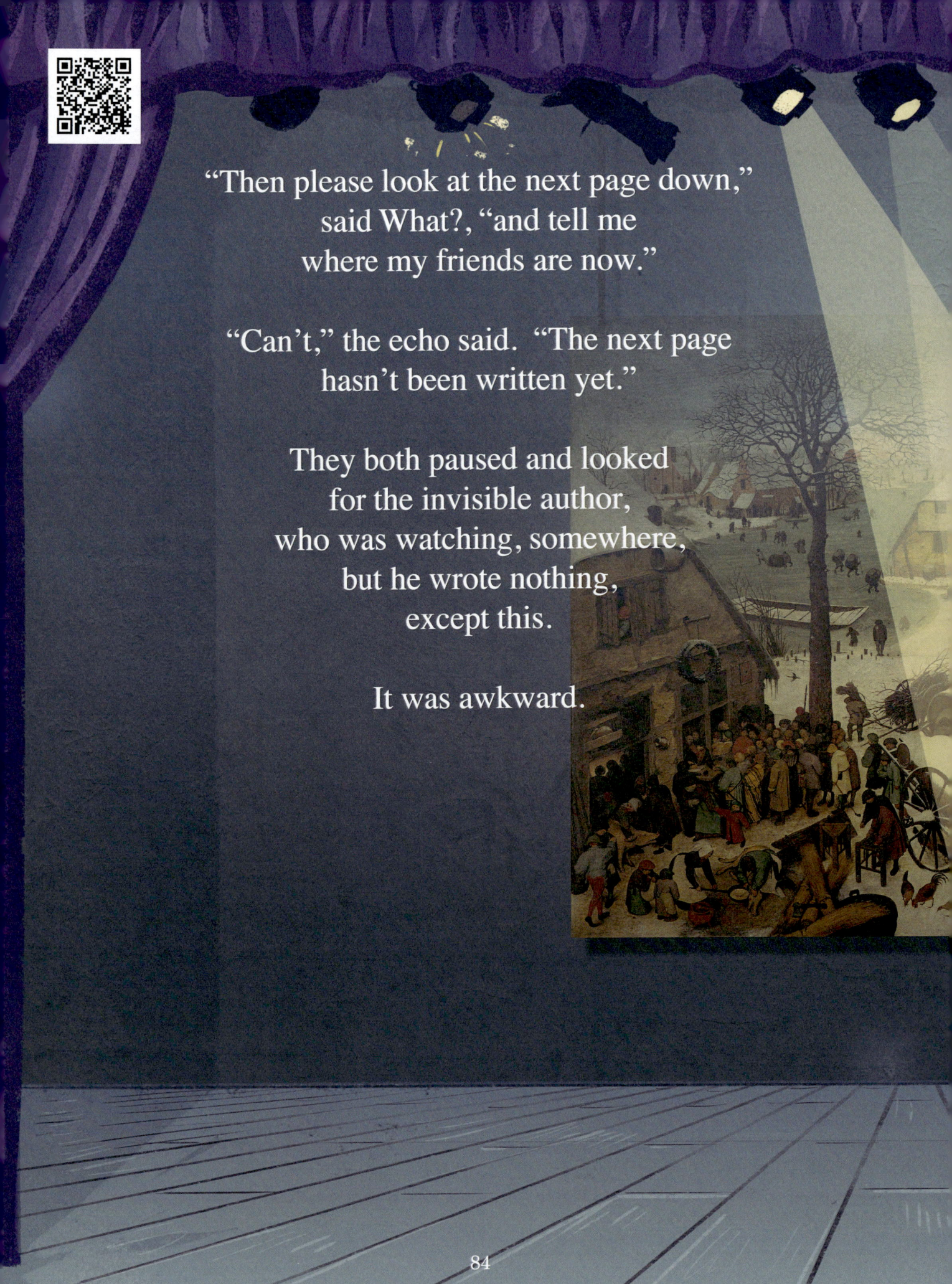

"Then please look at the next page down,"
said What?, "and tell me
where my friends are now."

"Can't," the echo said. "The next page
hasn't been written yet."

They both paused and looked
for the invisible author,
who was watching, somewhere,
but he wrote nothing,
except this.

It was awkward.

What? looked around the silent stage.

The big Brueghel prop hung silent
at the back, in shadow now.
What?'s friends were gone,
and he had to find them.

"Bye," he said.

"Bye," she echoed.

Off he jumped.

Act Four Review:
The Adjective Comma

We have already learned three comma rules. We learned to avoid the **subject/verb** and **compound word** commas and to put an **Oxford comma** in a list.

Now we discover a new rule about the **adjective comma**. It is another rule of unity: An adjective goes with its noun. Yay, unity! We would say that we saw a *red sunset*, not a *red, sunset*. If there are two adjectives before a noun, we might put a comma after the first one, such as in *It was a dark, cold sunset*. Here are some examples:

Yes: Burgull was a good monster.

Yes: Burgull was a sweet, good monster.

No: Burgull was a good, monster.

This way, the adjective is absorbed into the noun and modifies the vision of the noun, as all good adjectives do. The adjective and noun are a unity.

Act Four Practice Sentences

For each sentence, write *yes* if the sentence is correct and *no* if the sentence is not correct.

1. Poodle had a different, idea.

2. Poodle, had a different idea.

3. Poodle had a nap, and a walk.

4. Poodle likes snacks, tea, and cookies.

5. Poodle had a new idea.

6. Burgull ate beets, carrots and sandwiches.

7. Burgull, ate the new carrots.

8. Burgull ate the new, carrots.

9. Gawk liked dogs, and cats, and mice.

10. Gawk, and he saw birds, bugs, and blimps.

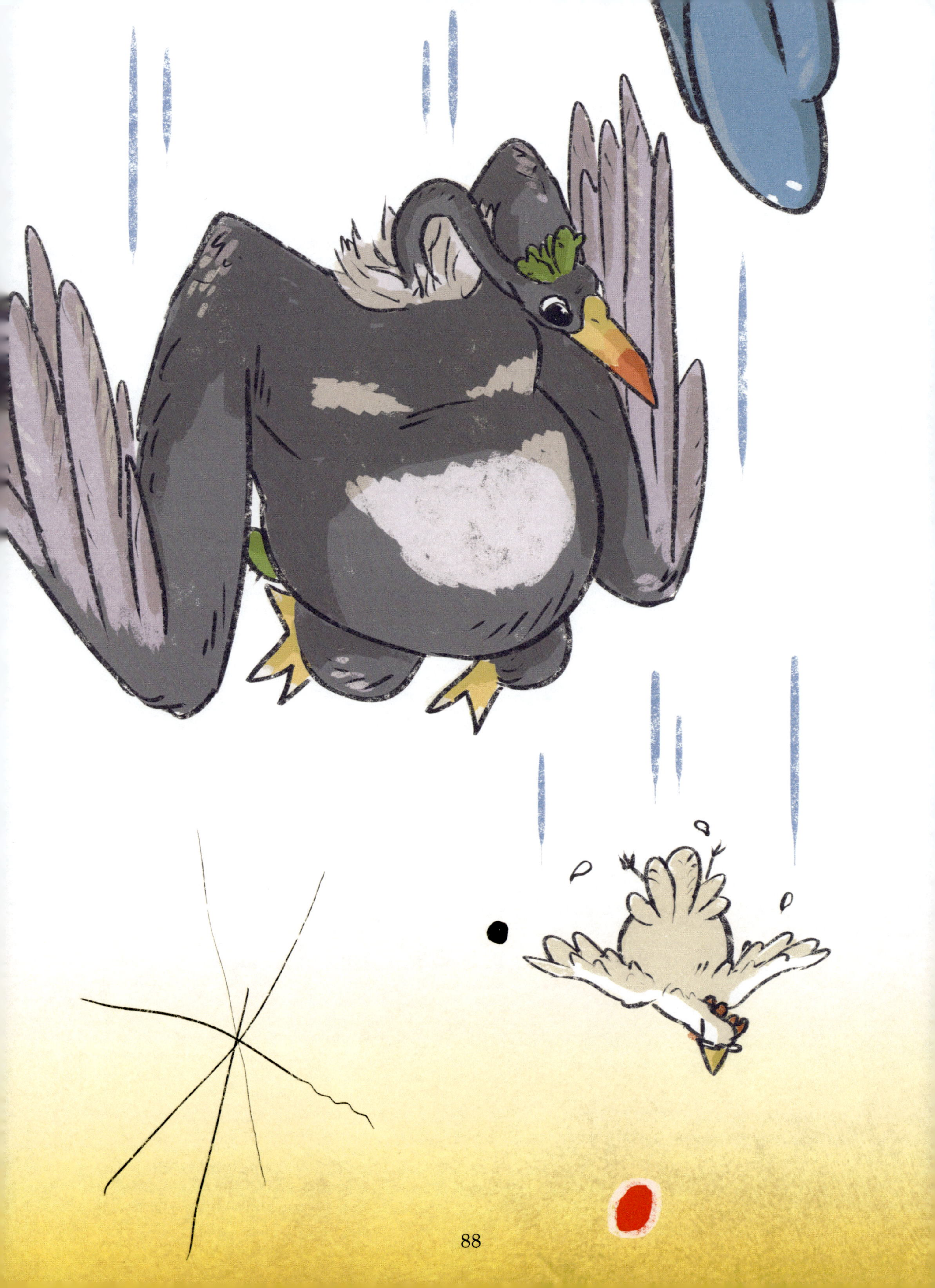

Act Five:
Miró

As What? dropped from the Brueghel,
his friends were falling too, far from view,
facing the wrong direction.
He was behind them.

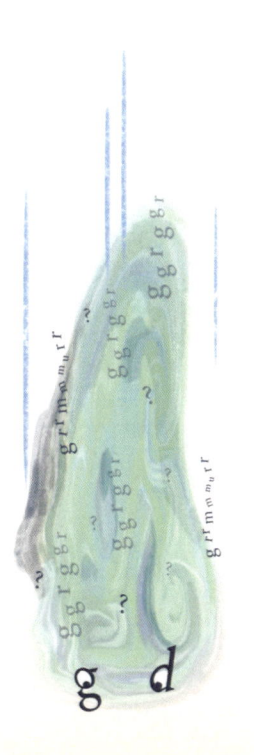

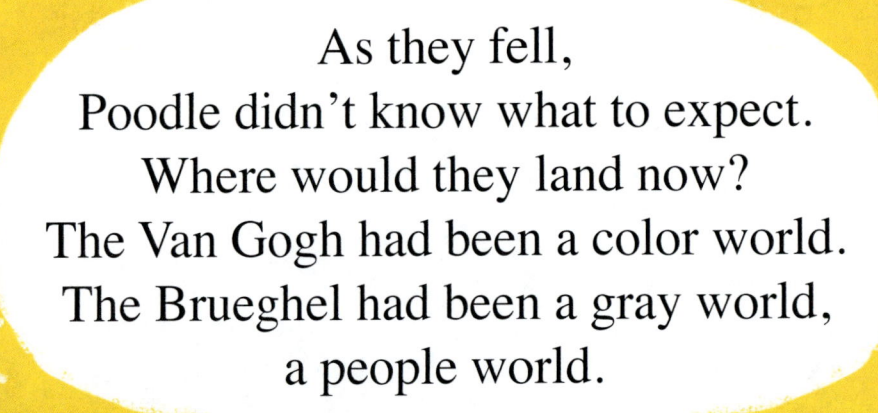

As they fell,
Poodle didn't know what to expect.
Where would they land now?
The Van Gogh had been a color world.
The Brueghel had been a gray world,
a people world.

In those paintings,
Poodle found different ways to think,
like stars winking on
in the sky of his mind.

But where would they land next?

They would know soon enough
because the bottom was zooming up,
so they aimed their feet
and braced for impact.
POOOOFFF!

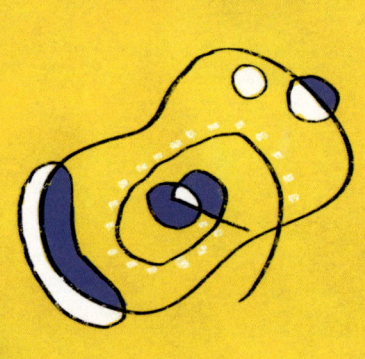

They shook their heads,
gained their balance,
and collected their wits.
(One wit escaped.)

"We have to stop landing like this," said Poodle.

They looked around.
This world was even more different
than the Van Gogh or the Brueghel!

"What in the world?" asked Sidney.

"Exactly," thought Poodle.

They had landed in a painted wild-world
of abstract forms, not like the sky,
not like a landscape, not like a sandwich,
not like anything they knew,
a kids' world, a playground of pure shapes,
of the inner fun of the world,
of circles and dots and lines,
of the secret geometry of reality,
of the design inside reality.

It was the world
as crayons would imagine it.
Crayons are so clever.

The colors were pure, like the Van Gogh,
and the scene was complex, like the Brueghel,
but this painting was different.

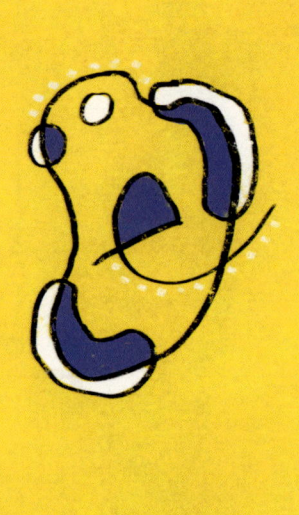

"Good grief," said Gawk.

They stood on a yellow plain,
or was it a plane?

All about, round shapes hovered near,
black blobs, red dots, a blue sphere,
and black strings stretched across here,
vibrating, seeking connections.

It was like standing in an atom.
It was different.

"I know what this is," said Poodle.
"This is a Miró."

"What?" asked the three monsters in unison.
They had been practicing.

"Miró," Poodle said. "Joan Miró."
He looked at his friends.
"We're in the mind of Miró.
Miró painted pure colors and forms—
his ideas of the pure secrets
that the truth is made of.
He painted ideas, not objects."

It was stunning.

Burgull bumped over to Poodle.
"Burgull like colors, Burgull like shapes," he said.

"Good, Burgull," said Poodle, "but don't put a comma
between two sentences or clauses that way.
That's called a **comma splice**.
You can't splice two clauses with a comma.
(Every **clause** has a subject and verb.)
Make two sentences, or add a conjunction, like this:"

Burgull likes colors. **Burgull likes** shapes.
Burgull likes colors, **and Burgull likes** shapes.

"Grbrkrrf?"

"See?" said Poodle. "No comma splices,
no subject/verb commas,
no compound word commas,
and no adjective/noun commas.
Put an Oxford comma in a list.
See? Pretty rules."

"Gbrffrg," Burgull offered.
He was beginning to understand.

"CUT!" cried Maybe,
storming from the curtain stage right.
Bizzie hurried after her,
looking back at something backstage.

"Author," Maybe called,
"did you write this comma stuff?
No more commas! Enough!
Focus on the story! Be tough!
What?'s lost, remember?
The friends have to search
the Miró for What?."

"Ah, well," the author began,
"I like commas, and I think commas—"

"Like commas? Stop! Please!" cried Maybe.
"What?'s lost, and we have to find him.
Concentrate! Where is he? Do you know?"

"Well, um, not yet," the author started.

"WHAT?!" cried Maybe. "You're the author,
and you don't know where What? is?"

"Well," said the author, "I haven't finished
this chapter yet, so—"

"Wait," Poodle interrupted,
"do you want me
to finish this chapter?
I can write it.
I can even write your lines, author."

"No!" Maybe cried. "Absolutely not!
Characters can't write authors' lines.
Nonsense!
Let's get back to finding What?."

Finally, something Sidney agreed with.

"Let's go, Maybe," said Sidney.

"Right," said Maybe. "ACTION!"
And she stormed off the stage,
Bizzie puffing after.

"Cut the lights!" Bizzie cried, breathless,
as she vanished behind the curtain.

Joe cut the lights,
and the wooden stage became the Miró,
and the yellow set became the land,
blooming like a flower.

Sidney looked at Miró-world.
This was different,
this yellow world
with floating objects.
Imaginary objects.
"Right," she said.
"Let's search the forms
and see if What?'s here."

And that is what they did.

Each friend had an assignment.

Poodle checked the blobs.

Dickinson searched the high things that reminded him of Blue Mountain.

Gawk soared over the yellow plain, or plane, scanning for What?. He had the sharpest eye. I mean, he's a hawk.

Burgull checked the stringy lines that reminded him of consonants. The consonants were his favorite.

Sidney zoomed and zipped, left and right, zoom puffs floating behind her.

Finally, they met
on a great blue globe floating in space,
and they gazed over the yellow place,
the plain, or plane—you decide.
What?? No trace.

The blue globe rolled, slow,
and they kept stepping sideways
to keep from slipping off.

From that blue vantage,
they saw the whole yellow page,
the whole imagined world,
from the left margin to the right margin.

They had looked everywhere.
No What?.

They were worried.
They had hurried.
They should have found What? by now.
They'd searched a Van Gogh,
and a Brueghel, and a Miró.
What? didn't show.
They'd have to jump again,
to a new painting.

"All right," sighed the author.
"I'll write one more painting."
The author was writing about himself
writing about himself.

"Let's get out of here," said Sidney,
and she jumped off the globe,
bounced on the yellow plain (or plane),
zoomed to the margin,
and leaped off the page,
and everyone chased her into the void.

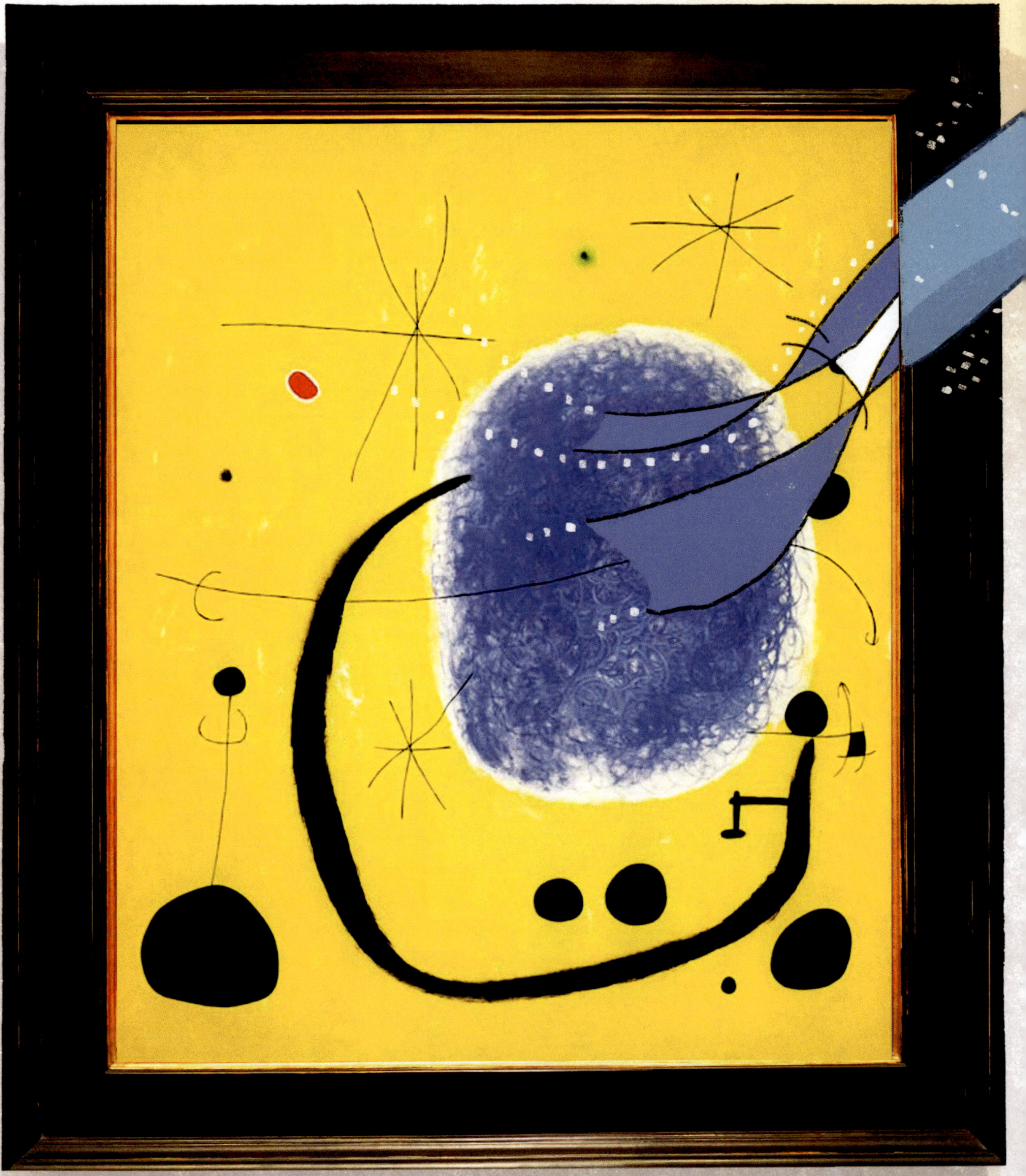

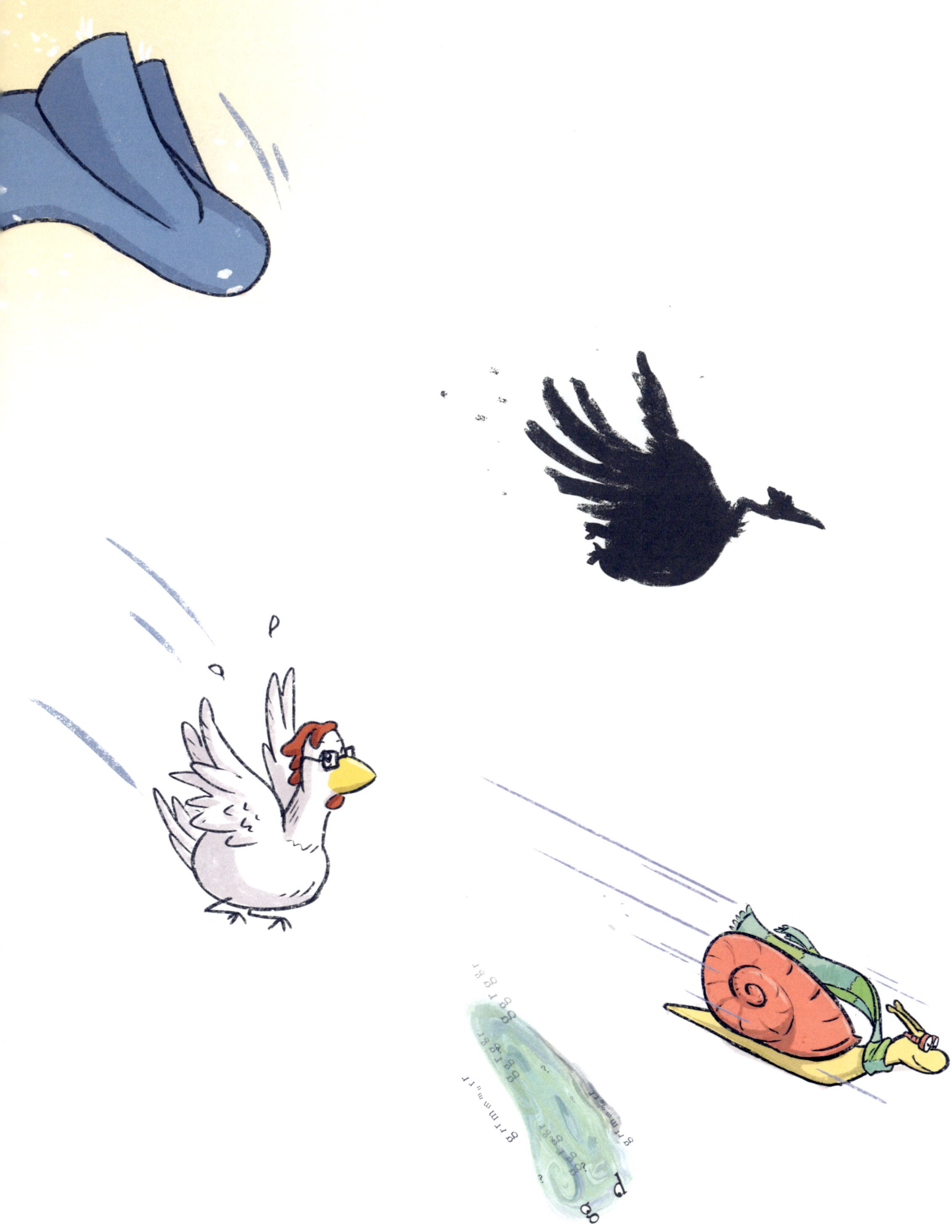

They were searching for What?,
who was even now dropping
toward the same page they were leaving,
about to land, bracing for impact,
four feet down.

And *poof!*,
What? landed on the now-empty stage
his friends had just left seconds before.
Already the Miró had faded,
and the blue and black props
were piled in the shadows
by the yellow curtain.

The theater was quiet,
except for you-know-who
fussing in the ceiling.

"Hello!" cried What?,
hoping his friends could hear him.
"What-what-what!" he barked.

"Well hello!" came an echo.

The author interrupted.
"I want a comma
after that interjection," he said.
"It should be '**Well, hello**!'
We always put a comma
after an **introductory interjection**."

"Wait," said the echo.
"I don't use commas. Ever.
I'm an echo. You only hear me.
You never see commas."

"I see them," said What?.

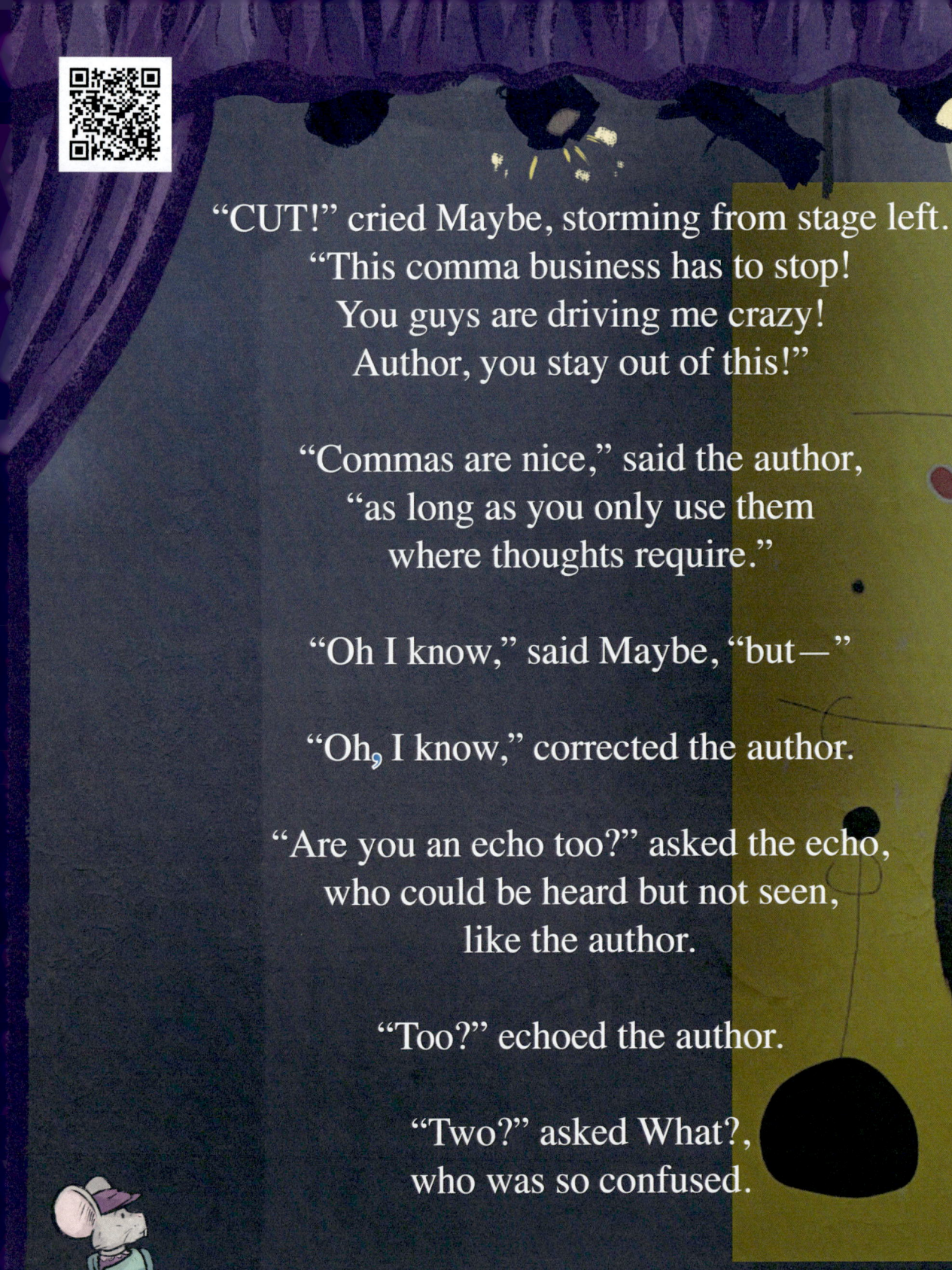

"CUT!" cried Maybe, storming from stage left.
"This comma business has to stop!
You guys are driving me crazy!
Author, you stay out of this!"

"Commas are nice," said the author,
"as long as you only use them
where thoughts require."

"Oh I know," said Maybe, "but—"

"Oh, I know," corrected the author.

"Are you an echo too?" asked the echo,
who could be heard but not seen,
like the author.

"Too?" echoed the author.

"Two?" asked What?,
who was so confused.

"Stop this at once!" cried Maybe.
"What?, go find your friends. Jump!
Joe, cut the lights! ACTION!"
And off the stage she stormed.

And with that,
What? jumped off the page
he had just reached. He knew
he was gaining on his friends.
He could almost hear their echoes
bounding 'round the stage.
"I'll catch them," he thought,
"in the next chapter."

Act Five Review:
The Clause Comma

We have learned four comma rules already, and they make sentences beautiful. We have learned about the **subject/verb** comma, the **compound word** comma, the **Oxford** comma, and the **adjective** comma.

Now we discover a fifth idea that lets a comma keep two ideas separate and clear. The comma goes between two **clauses** that are joined by a conjunction. A clause is a group of words that contains a subject and a predicate. For example:

Burgull was a monster**, and Poodle ate** a chicken.

See the two clauses in blue? The subjects/verbs are *Burgull/was* and *Poodle/ate*. It is like two sentences in one. We call this structure a **compound sentence**, and in it you must have the comma or else you have a **run-on sentence**:

No: Burgull was a monster **and Poodle was** a chicken.

Ugh, right? It is all mixed together. The first idea runs on into the second idea. We need that compound sentence comma.

Act Five Practice Sentences

For each sentence, write *yes* if the sentence is correct and *no* if the sentence is not correct.

1. Burgull leaped, and Sidney fell.

2. Burgull jumped at the blue, sphere.

3. Burgull had apples, oranges, and pears.

4. Burgull, ate two beets.

5. Burgull ate beets, and pears.

6. Burgull ate beets and pears, and Poodle sat.

7. Burgull and Poodle, ate no beets.

8. Burgull saw Poodle, and Gawk.

9. Burgull, always wanted to eat beets.

10. Burgull ate beets and Poodle ate soup.

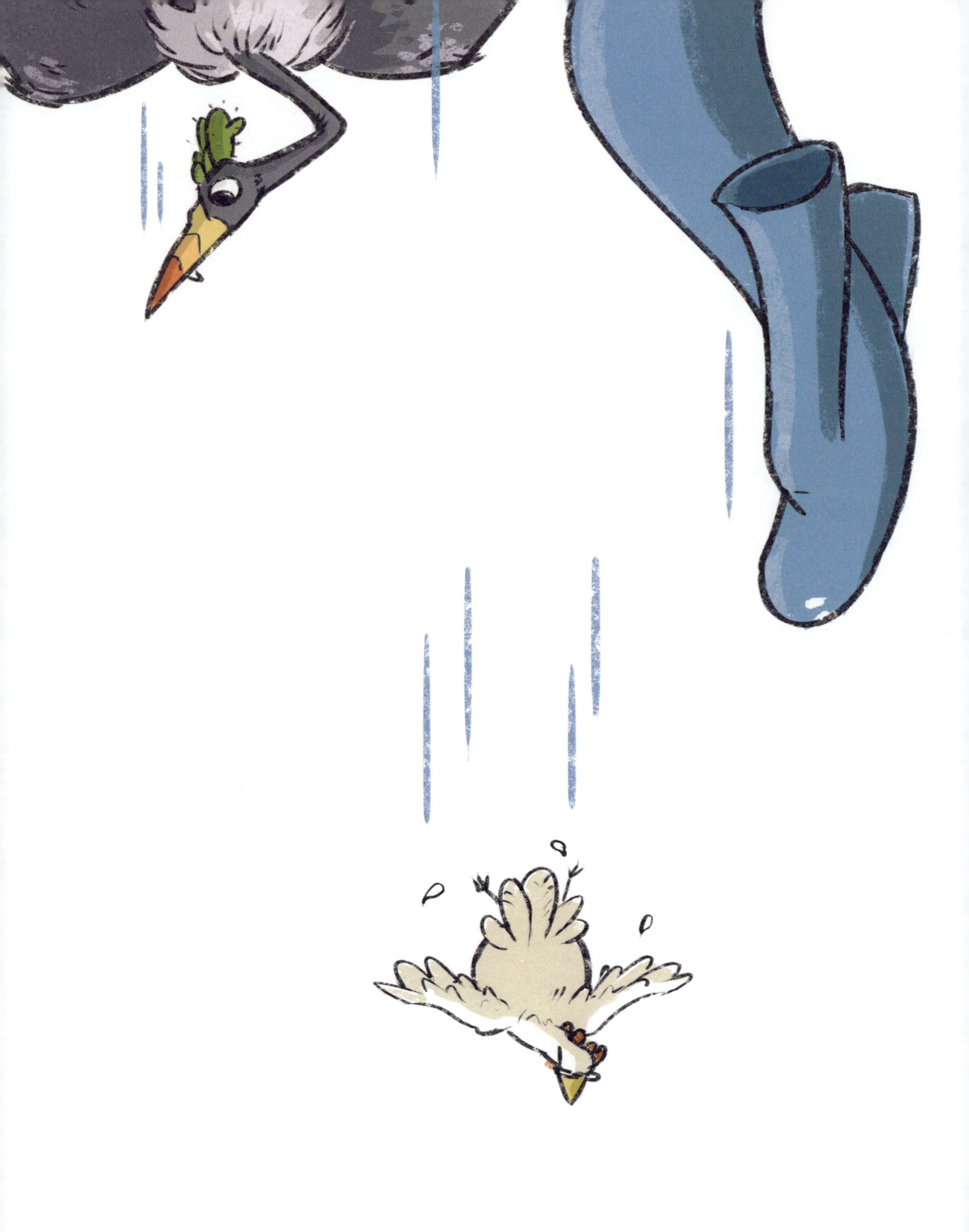

Act Six:
Vermeer

As What? plummeted from the Miró,
his friends were falling too, far below him,
determined to find him.

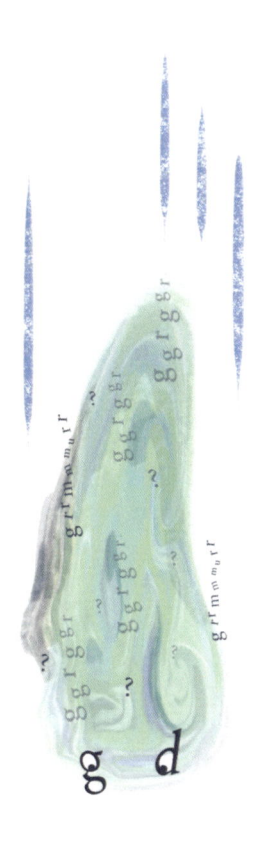

They fell, and they fell,
through a tempest,
past cloud-capped towers,
through a sentence, past gorgeous palaces,
past a dentist, past solemn temples,
past an apprentice, past the great globe,
and they fell past paragraphs,
past Long John Silver,
past commas that buzzed out fussing.
They fell past years, past centuries.
The blue whiz marks dashed down
after them like crazy, but they were slower
than shadows and could never catch up.
Shadows are like lightning.

Whiz marks have it tough.

Sidney's whiz marks, especially,
could not keep up. She's too speedy.

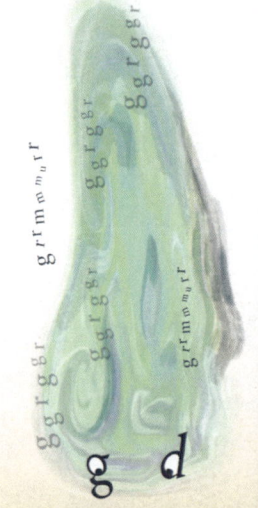

One child, high above the book,
said, "Whew," took off
her glasses, and thought,
"They'll land in a new painting
with a poof!"

Which, of course, they did.
She was right. Kids know.

"*Poof!*" said the landing,
as required.

They had landed in a room!

But not just any room.

With the *poof* still ringing,
they shook themselves, wringing,
collected their wits — all but one —
and looked around.
This *was* different.

They were standing in a painting
behind a painted painter
in the painting who was painting a lady in blue.
The painted room was beautiful,
with soft light streaming from the left edge.
A tapestry map of the Netherlands
and Belgium hung on the wall.

"But wait," Poodle thought,
"this is a painting of the painter painting.
It's not a painting of the woman."

Yes, the painter with his back to them
was a painted painter painting a painted woman,
painted by the painter who painted him painting her.

What?
(Not the dog, just the question.)

"Where are we?" whispered Sidney.
She didn't want to interrupt the painter—
the painted one.
He was so intense.

"I know this," said Poodle.
"We're in a Vermeer.
See those bubbles of light?"

"Vermeer?" asked Dickinson.

"Yes," Poodle said. "A Dutch painter.
We must be in 1666 Holland.
I remember this painting.
It's called *The Art of Painting*."

"Why did you put the painting title
in italics?" asked Gawk.

"That's what you do," Poodle told him.

They gathered close and peeked
at the painted painting painter's painting.
He was painting the woman as a muse, Clio,
one of the nine Olympian muses
of ancient Greek mythology.
You knew she was Clio because
she wore a blue laurel wreath,
and she held a history book
and a trumpet.

"This is beautiful," Poodle said.

"Thank you," came some voice from somewhere.

They looked around. Who said that?

"Was that you?" asked Poodle,
whispering over the painted painter's shoulder.

"No," the painted painter replied.
"That's Vermeer. He does that.
He painted me in here, and now I'm older.
I've been sitting here for four hundred years,
working on this laurel wreath."

Poodle did not dare to comment.
"Where is Vermeer?" he asked, looking about.

"Up there somewhere," said the painted painter,
gesturing toward the ceiling.
"I don't know where he is. I never see him.
I just appear as he paints me,
like fog condensing on a leaf."

"I wrote him," said the author's voice suddenly. "I wrote Vermeer into this book."

"Wrong," said Vermeer's voice from somewhere. "I painted this scene, and you're in it."

"I wrote you," said the author.

"I painted you," said Vermeer.

They both spoke from somewhere.

"Oh, brother," said a child in the balcony. Kids will only stand for so much.

"CUT!" cried Maybe,
storming in from stage right,
Bizzie scurrying behind.

"This is my *play*!" Maybe cried. "Remember that!
This is my stage, and I direct this script.
Let's keep our concepts straight!"

"No," said the author, "your play is in this book
that I wrote. I wrote your play. I wrote you too.
You're just a character of mine. You're me.
All of you are just sentences of mine."

"Wrong," came Vermeer's voice.
"I painted this act.
This room came from my brush."

"Author," said Maybe, "you stay out of this.
Vermeer, you too. It's my play."

"In my book," said the author.

"Oh, brother," thought the child.

"Oh, brother," echoed an echo from somewhere.
Echoes always agree with kids. Period.

"Enough of this," said Sidney,
who always knew what was important.
"Let's search this place and find What?."

"Right," said the monsters in perfect harmony.
They had been practicing, without acrimony,
like crooning monsters.

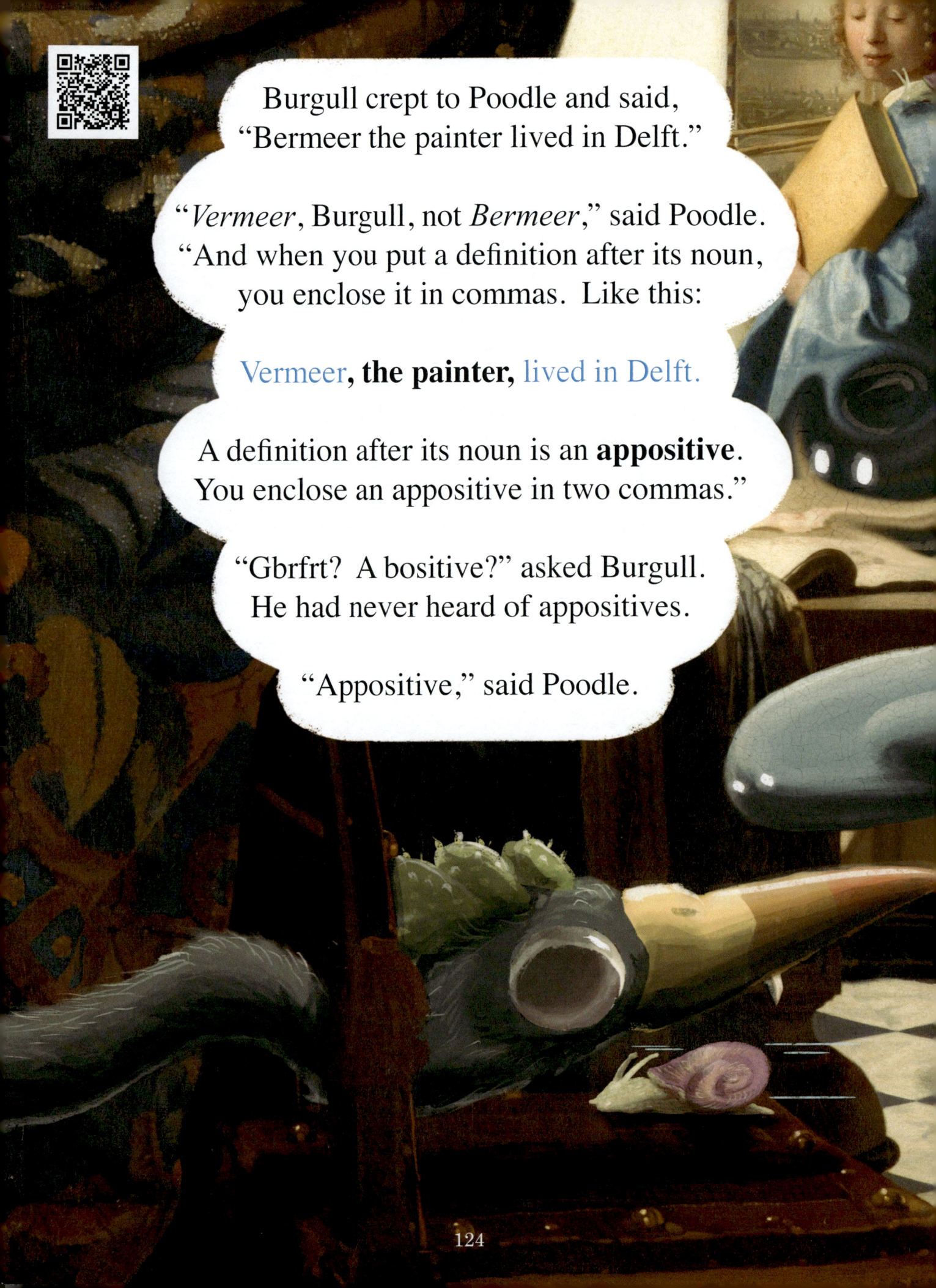

Burgull crept to Poodle and said, "Bermeer the painter lived in Delft."

"*Vermeer*, Burgull, not *Bermeer*," said Poodle. "And when you put a definition after its noun, you enclose it in commas. Like this:

Vermeer**, the painter,** lived in Delft.

A definition after its noun is an **appositive**. You enclose an appositive in two commas."

"Gbrfrt? A bositive?" asked Burgull. He had never heard of appositives.

"Appositive," said Poodle.

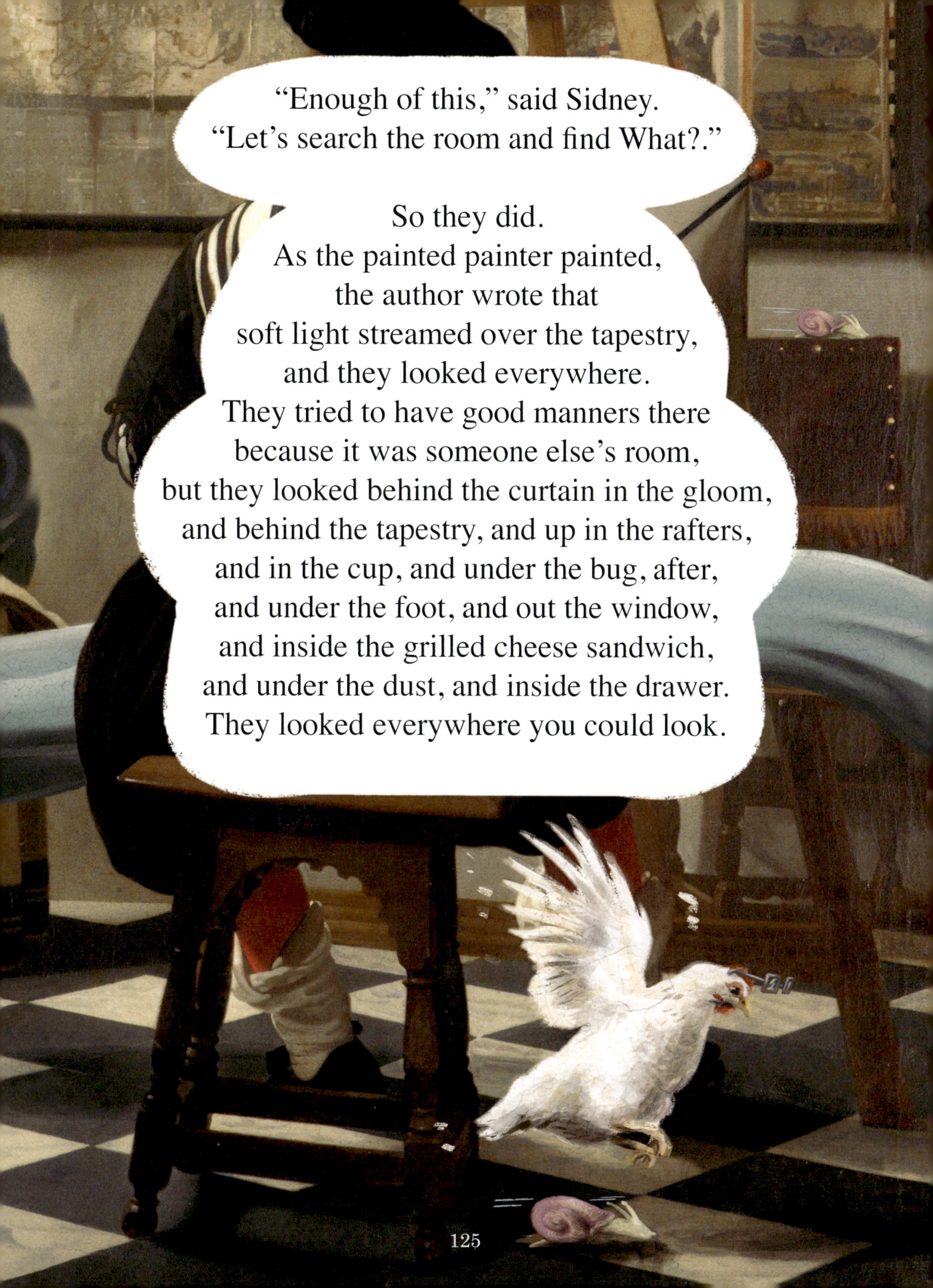

"Enough of this," said Sidney.
"Let's search the room and find What?."

So they did.
As the painted painter painted,
the author wrote that
soft light streamed over the tapestry,
and they looked everywhere.
They tried to have good manners there
because it was someone else's room,
but they looked behind the curtain in the gloom,
and behind the tapestry, and up in the rafters,
and in the cup, and under the bug, after,
and under the foot, and out the window,
and inside the grilled cheese sandwich,
and under the dust, and inside the drawer.
They looked everywhere you could look.

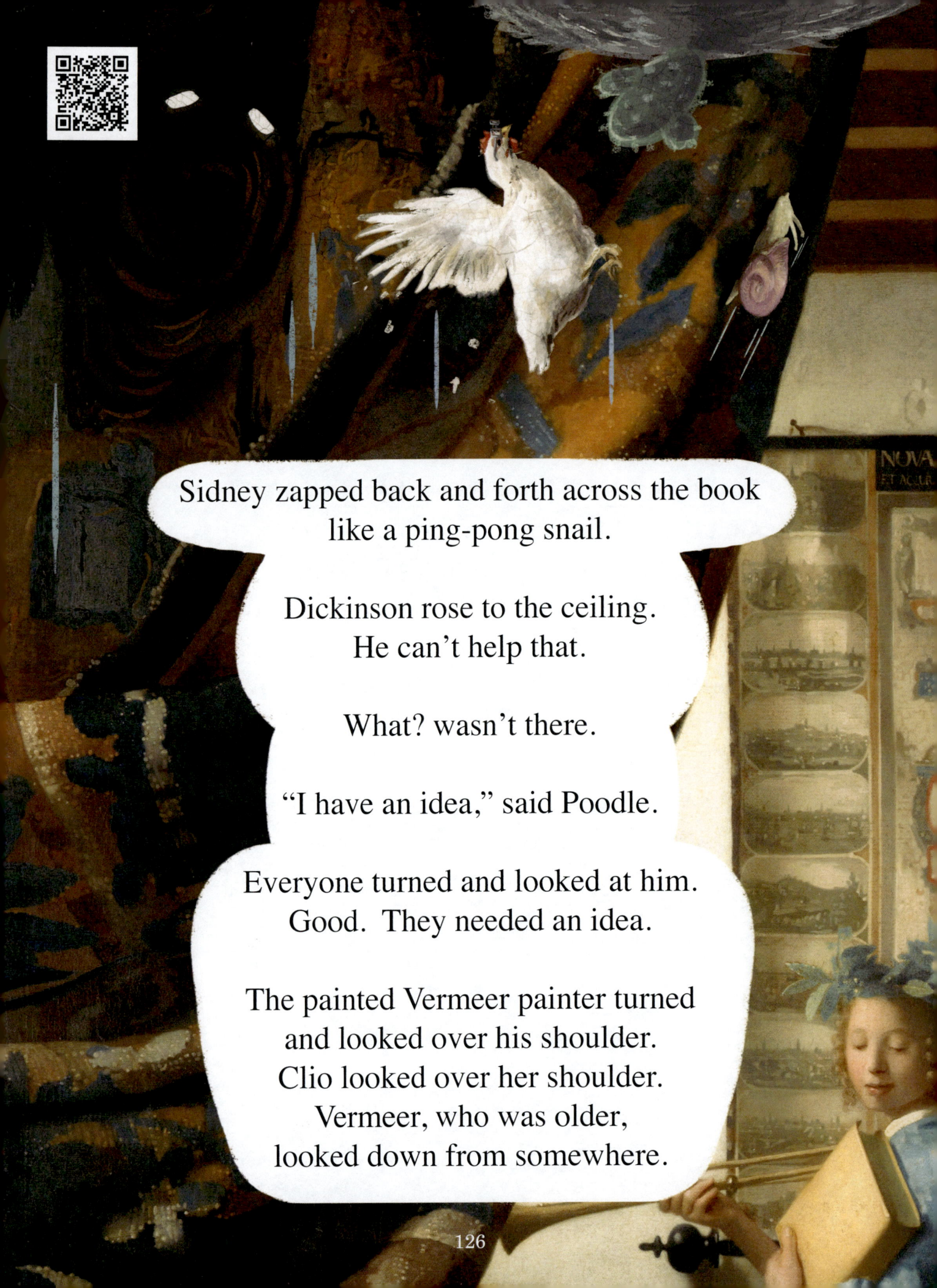

Sidney zapped back and forth across the book
like a ping-pong snail.

Dickinson rose to the ceiling.
He can't help that.

What? wasn't there.

"I have an idea," said Poodle.

Everyone turned and looked at him.
Good. They needed an idea.

The painted Vermeer painter turned
and looked over his shoulder.
Clio looked over her shoulder.
Vermeer, who was older,
looked down from somewhere.

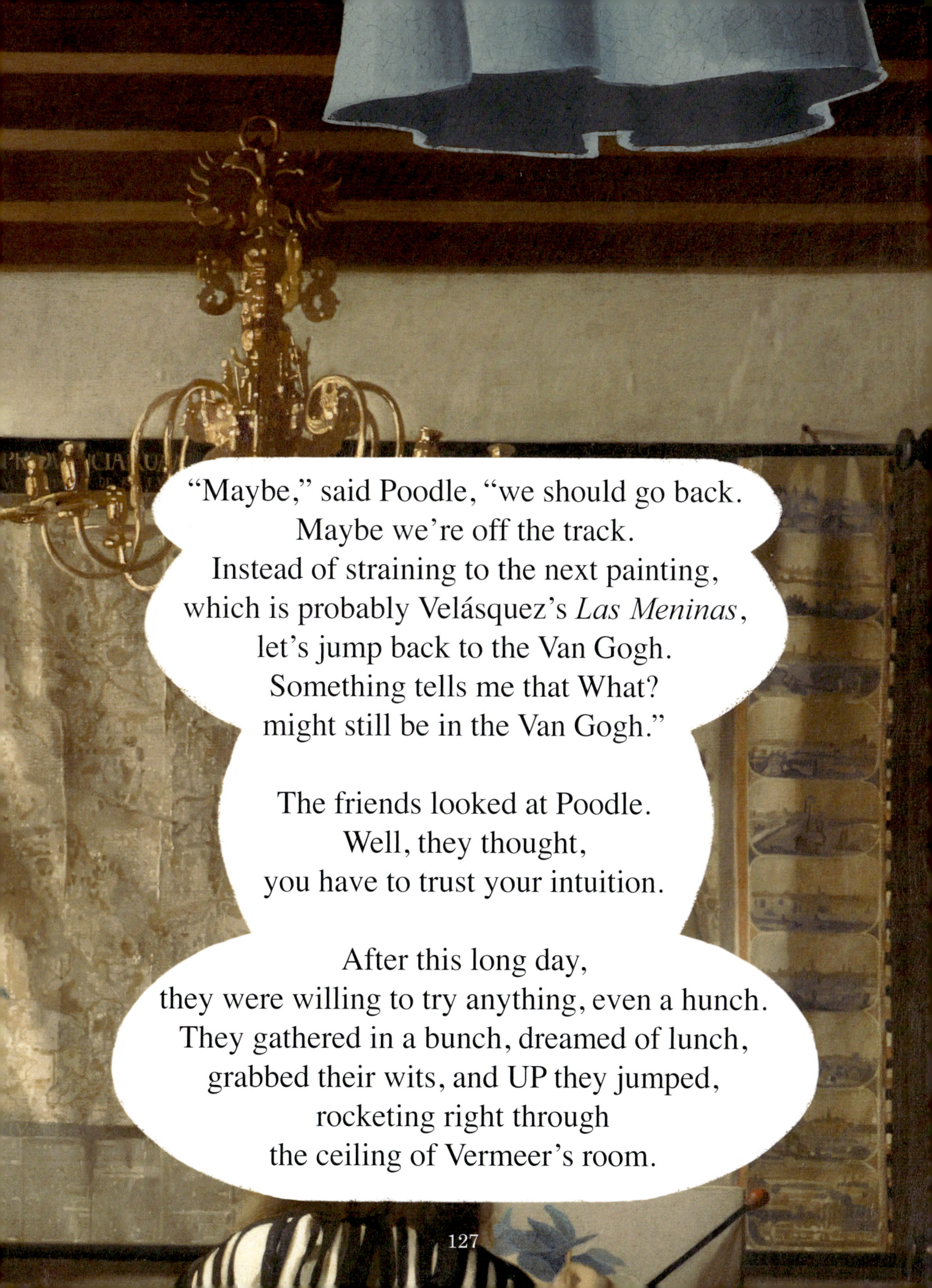

"Maybe," said Poodle, "we should go back.
Maybe we're off the track.
Instead of straining to the next painting,
which is probably Velásquez's *Las Meninas*,
let's jump back to the Van Gogh.
Something tells me that What?
might still be in the Van Gogh."

The friends looked at Poodle.
Well, they thought,
you have to trust your intuition.

After this long day,
they were willing to try anything, even a hunch.
They gathered in a bunch, dreamed of lunch,
grabbed their wits, and UP they jumped,
rocketing right through
the ceiling of Vermeer's room.

As they ascended,
streaking up from the Vermeer to the Miró,
who should they see descending past them
but What?, who was dropping like a stone
from the Miró to the Vermeer!
They crossed like spaceships at night.
Friends up, What? down!

"What?!!!!" the friends cried as he blasted past them.

"What-what-what-what-what!" What? barked
as they shot up above him.

Finally, they had found one another!
The long trek was over.
Their hearts were filled with joy.

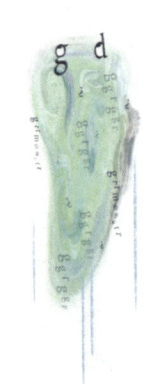

"Meet us in the Van Gogh!" cried Poodle to What?,
who was now a vanishing spot way down there.

"What-what-what!" came the grffy reply.

So, after much jumping up,
from the Vermeer up to the Miró,
then up to the Brueghel, then up to the Van Gogh,
boing boing boing,
they finally stuck their *poofs*—
even What?, who arrived last.

It was a great reunion,
with hugs and back-claps and jokes
and burgly consonants.
And high above them,
the massive Van Gogh starry night
swirled and glittered and winked.

Poodle was so happy to see his pal again,
and the monsters did their monster dance,
toes left, toes right, doot-de-doo,
and Sidney ran some zippy zap.

Burgull stole over to Poodle. He whispered,
"Gawk said "We found What?."

"A comma," Poodle said.
"You need a **quote comma**
before the quote. It should be:

Gawk said, "We found What?."

"See? To separate the speaker from what is spoken."

"Gbrrfr?" asked Burgull.

As the happy friends celebrated their reunion
with yippees and woohoos,
they stood together and looked up
at the boundless Van Gogh,
swirling with bold truths,
and thought how lucky they were
to live in such a starry night.

Poodle thought about what he'd learned
from the paintings he'd seen,
from the colors of Van Gogh,
from the lives in Brueghel,
from the forms of Miró,
from the artist painting himself in Vermeer.
Each painting had a different idea, a new light,
and Poodle's mind felt open and bright.
He felt that he could take in more now.
The paintings had made his mind roomy.

Poodle thought, though, that he would say
one more thing to Burgull about commas....

"CUT!" cried Maybe, storming onto the stage,
with Bizzie hurrying behind,
glancing at Poodle as she passed.
"CUT! LIGHTS! I know what you're doing, Poodle!
No you don't! No more commas! Enough is enough!
Leave sweet Burgull alone, and call it a day.
Snack time, everyone!"

She stormed off.
You know how she storms.

Bizzie looked at Poodle.
"We can talk about my name,"
she whispered, "in the next book."
And she wisped away.

Joe turned the grumpy lights on.

With that, they sat on the edge of the stage,
and fished in their sandwich pockets
for their favorite sandwiches,
and dangled their legs
over the stage, and wiggled their toes,
and munched sandwiches they chose,
and talked about paintings, like pros,
or thought about thinking,
or remembered something—who knows?—
or just smiled at the audience,
who sat there, happy,
enjoying the closing act.

And high above them, very high,
from the left margin all the way to the right margin,
Van Gogh's universe put on a show.

      The End

Act Six Review:
The Quote Comma

We have learned that good commas make sentences beautiful. We have learned about the **subject/verb** comma, the **compound word** comma, the **Oxford** comma, the **adjective** comma, and the **clause** comma.

Now we discover a final rule that provides a good introduction to a quotation. For example:

> **Poodle said, "Burgull is one of my best friends."**

See how the commas give each part of the idea its own identity? Here is another:

> **Dickinson said, "I miss Blue Mountain."**

Notice that the final period goes INSIDE the quotation marks.

Nice, eh?

Act Six Practice Sentences

For each sentence, write *yes* if the sentence is correct and *no* if the sentence is not correct.

1. Burgull said "I like that painting."

2. Burgull, ate no beets.

3. Burgull likes Van Gogh, Brueghel, and Miró.

4. Burgull saw the old, noodle.

5. Burgull likes noodles, beets and pie.

6. Burgull, ran to the margin.

7. Burgull saw Dickinson, Poodle, and Sidney.

8. Burgull replied, "I like more paintings."

9. Burgull, never asked for anything.

10. Burgull wanted the old map again.

End of Book Quiz

For each pair of sentences, choose the one that is correct.

1.   a. Gurff always ate glurbs, and kleebs.
     b. Gurff always ate glurbs and kleebs.

2.   a. In 2018 Gurff ate no pie.
     b. In 2018 Gurff, ate no pie.

3.   a. Gurff seldom saw giraffes, gerbils, or greebs.
     b. Gurff seldom saw giraffes, gerbils or greebs.

4.   a. Gurff saw weevils and Mort heard weevils.
     b. Gurff saw weevils, and Mort heard weevils.

5.   a. Gurff replied, "Yes, I have no bananas."
     b. Gurff replied "Yes, I have no bananas."

6.   a. The friendly Gurff, knew no weevil.
     b. The friendly Gurff knew no weevil.

7.   a. Gurff, and Mort agreed about weevils.
     b. Gurff and Mort agreed about weevils.

8. a. Gurff liked momos, lolos, and fofos.
    b. Gurff liked momos, lolos and fofos.

9. a. Gurff turned and said "No, no giraffes."
    b. Gurff turned and said, "No, no giraffes."

10. a. Gurff liked blue, and Mort liked green.
    b. Gurff liked blue and Mort liked green.

11. a. Gurff, rapidly ate the raw beets.
    b. Gurff rapidly ate the raw beets.

12. a. Gurff frowned at the beets, and feet.
    b. Gurff frowned at the beets and feet.

13. a. Gurff sang do, re, and mi.
    b. Gurff sang do, re and mi.

14. a. Gurff said, "Blurf, I presume."
    b. Gurff said "Blurf, I presume."

15. a. Gurff gargled but Murp googled.
    b. Gurff gargled, but Murp googled.

16. a. Gurff, almost always fluffed.
    b. Gurff almost always fluffed.

17. a. Gurff gawked and loomed alone.

 b. Gurff gawked, and loomed alone.

18. a. Gurff ate biscuits, baskets and burgers

 b. Gurff ate biscuits, baskets, and burgers.

19. a. Gurff saw the baggy buffoon.

 b. Gurff saw the baggy, buffoon.

20. a. Gurff and Murp never knew the news.

 b. Gurff, and Murp never knew the news.